Lucky Bamboo
Book of Crafts
吉祥竹手工大全

Written and Illustrated
by Jennifer DeCristoforo

This book is dedicated to Cloe, 我爱你

Library of Congress Cataloging-in-Publication Data
DeCristoforo, Jennifer.
  Lucky bamboo book of crafts / Jennifer DeCristoforo.
  p. cm.
  ISBN 978-0-9884648-0-3
  Includes bibliographic references and index.

  1. Handicraft – China – Juvenile literature. 2. China – Social life and customs – Juvenile literature. I. DeCristoforo, Jennifer. II. Title.

  TT160.D328 2013
  745.5 – dc23

                                        2012919259

Design and Production:
Frank Berté Jr., Destin Interactive
Emma Lockwood, Emma Lockwood Graphic Design

Photo: 'About the Author' portrait by Nance Trueworthy

Printed in Singapore by CraftPrint International Ltd.
10 9 8 7 6 5 4 3 2 1

Please note:
The project instructions in this book include sharp, toxic and potentially dangerous supplies. Please use extreme caution, supervision and safety practices with children. The author and those involved in publishing Lucky Bamboo Book of Crafts take no responsibility for personal safety while using this book.

Author's note:
The information in this book has been thoroughly researched to the fullest accuracy possible. However in some instances there are differing historical accounts. Also, projects have been adapted from traditional methods, but often do not entirely replicate them. The author/publisher will not assume liability for damages caused by inaccuracies in the data, and makes no warranty on the accuracy of the information contained herein.

For inquiries and orders:
http://www.luckybamboocrafts.com   e-mail: info@luckybamboocrafts.com
Lucky Bamboo Crafts, P.O. Box 1022, Yarmouth, ME 04096

Table of Contents

TRADITIONAL FINE ARTS 传统艺术

FESTIVALS & HOLIDAYS 节日和假日

PERFORMANCE & DANCE 表演和舞蹈

Table of Contents
continued

REPRODUCIBLE DESIGNS & GUIDES

CHINESE CULTURE RESOURCE PAGES

About the Author

Ni Hao!

I am Jennifer DeCristoforo, the author, illustrator, editor, and most significant contributor to all other aspects of this book. Lucky Bamboo Book of Crafts has been my labor of love for several years and here is why it was born.

I have a background in many areas of the arts including illustration, design, art direction, elementary art education, educational publishing and product design. My passion for Chinese culture grew from early trips to Asia to supervise product development for my employer (when I often wished I could extend my stay), and later in a much more intimate context becoming the parent of my precious daughter Cloe Mei, adopted from Jiangxi, China in 2003.

Since Maine is our home, I'm always looking for ways to forge cultural connections with China and the Chinese-American community here. I'm involved with planning our Chinese New Year celebration each year and my daughter has attended our local Chinese school on weekends since she was a toddler.

I have written the book that I wished I had been able to find years ago, not only to have interesting craft instruction for Chinese holidays and special events but to share with my daughter a richer connection to her homeland as she grows up in a conspicuously non-diverse environment.

The challenge was to select and design a meaningful collection of craft projects within the vast history and significant cultural ingenuity of China. Not easy! But I also wanted it to be about having fun and being creative, so hopefully you will be inspired and educated by what you find in these pages and come away wanting to learn or share even more about China. This book is just a touchstone to the large and magnificent world of Chinese history, art, culture and crafts.

Xie xie!

All my best, Jennifer

How to Use This Book

These crafts are designed to be user-friendly for both individuals and groups. Each project instruction includes the following:

Description of Craft:
Here you will find general information on the Chinese origin, history and purpose of the craft item.

Skill Level:
This indicates the recommended age level of difficulty. You'll find the crafts appeal to all ages (including adults!) so they will work well at schools, fairs and events with multi-aged groups. This is just a guide, so keep in mind most of the crafts can be adapted to any age with adult supervision and simplifying some of the steps.

Level 1	Level 2	Level 3	Level 4
3-6 yrs.	6-9 yrs.	9-12 yrs.	12-15 yrs.

Tool Icons:
These are the tools that will be needed to make the project. They differ from the materials list as they are *tools* used to make the craft versus the actual *materials* in the construction. If you don't have everything handy, you can use what's available; for example, crayons or colored pencils instead of markers, white glue instead of a glue stick or staples instead of tape.

Scissors   Glue   Exacto   Hole Punch   Glue Stick   Pen   Stapler

Marker   Ruler   Pencil   Masking tape   Tape   Brush   Copier

Materials:
These are the materials to construct the particular craft as it is presented. Listed is what you'll need for one complete project, so like a recipe, you need to multiply the quantity per piece. As with the tools, you can sometimes come up with a swap out to use what you have available.

Steps:
These are the step-by-step instructions to follow. They coordinate with the numbered drawings for visual reference.

Did you Know?:
These are interesting and surprising "factoids" related to the project to enhance your crafting experience.

Keep in mind there are valuable resources throughout the book that educate about Chinese culture and lead you to more sources of information. All the projects will be more interesting, enriching and fun if you share some context for the activity!

Also Try:
This is a cross-reference for other projects in the book you may want to consider trying because of their common theme or a similarity.

Grain of Rice:
These are special tips to make your craft even more successful.

Traditional Fine Arts

传统艺术

TRADiTiONAL FiNE ARTS

CALLIGRAPHY STROKES
书法

Calligraphy is a very special traditional art of China. It is historically written using a brush and ink on a unique type of paper called Xuan paper that is made in China especially for this purpose, or on thin silk.

The written language of calligraphy symbols is the same across all the regions of China, even though there are thousands of dialects of spoken language. Chinese writing of characters goes back more than 3,000 years and is one of the oldest surviving written languages in the world. The first symbols began as pictures drawn to resemble the actual things they represented and gradually they changed to characters.

The earliest calligraphy appeared as inscriptions on bones and tortoise shells of the Shang Dynasty. In the Qin dynasty, after the First Emperor of Qin unified China, the unified characters improved the development of calligraphy. Through the Han, Tang, Jin, Song, and Ming dynasties, calligraphy became more and more sophisticated, especially in Tang dynasty which was the peak. There are different styles of calligraphy, including Zheng, Cao, Li, Zhuan, and Xing.

YOU'LL NEED:
• Asian style calligraphy brush or medium-sized paint brush with tapered point

MATERIALS:
• Xuan paper or any smooth rice or plant-based paper
• Paper towels
• Black ink (or) ink stick & stone
• Scrap or newspaper
• Water to clean up

STEPS:
1. Relax and prepare your area with paper, ink, brush and test paper. Study the order and direction of the five strokes

2. Load some ink on the tip of the brush and try some strokes on the scrap paper until you have the right weight of line and feel control. Try to hold your brush vertically from the surface

3. Move to your writing paper and smoothly apply your strokes one-by-one, slowly enough to maintain control but quickly enough to not pool your ink

GRAIN OF RICE

If you don't have calligraphy ink handy, use a children's watercolor box and moisten just the black pan to make a puddle that resembles ink

✱ See Resource Section p. 129 for some other common characters to practice

Traditional Fine Arts

传统艺术

STROKES:

Every Chinese character has several strokes.
These five fundamental strokes are the first that should be practiced:

1.

Héng
(horizontal dash)

2.

Shù
(vertical downstroke)

3.

Pie
(left downstroke)

4.

Dian
(dot)

5.

Zhé
(bend)

Did You Know?

+ In China, calligraphy or "beautiful writing" is said to reveal the artist's inner self. The "life" in each brush stroke not only displays skill and education, but also expresses personal traits and the beauty of one's soul

Write calligraphy of a favorite word or phrase you find with ink and brush or select one from the Resource Section. Then be inspired to create original artwork of the same theme.

You can work on the same paper or scroll, or mount the two separate finished pieces together on a decorative paper or light board. This art of expression has been done by Chinese masters for thousands of years.

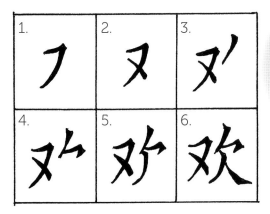

 Happy (huān)

ALSO TRY

Traditional Papermaking p. 20

Brush Painted Scroll p. 14

MING DYNASTY POTTERY

明代陶艺

China is the birthplace of the earliest pottery dating back over 10,000 years, and was how the term "china" for dishes became known. By the mid 1300's, Chinese ceramics became the most advanced in the world, with most pieces made from fine "porcelain" clay. They were usually decorated with natural or symbolic subjects such as the phoenix, dragon, flower designs or landscapes.

During the time of the Ming Dynasty (1368-1644) there was a huge advance in artistic techniques, ceramic designs and firing kilns which allowed China to lead in creating and exporting Ming ceramics and porcelain.

Many believe the first true porcelain came from Zhejiang Province where the earliest porcelain kiln sites have been found. Porcelain is made from clay and stone and is white, smooth and even translucent when very thin and is fired at very high temperatures. The northeastern part of Jiangxi Province is now known as the porcelain center of China for modern production. However ancient "Ming vases" and many other Ming vessels, objects and found fragments remain priceless collectibles in museums today.

With this easy air-dry method you can make your own clay, sculpt your bowl and paint it with a Chinese design. If you get more experienced with ceramics and have access to a supervised studio and kiln, you can try porcelain clay on a potter's wheel and then fire your piece just as the ancient Chinese did.

YOU'LL NEED:

- 2 paint brushes- medium and very small bristle
- Brush rinsing container
- Measuring cup
- Bowl

GRAIN OF RICE

A clear glazing coat can be applied to the finished bowl for a "porcelain" shine. Extra clay can be stored in a plastic bag in the refrigerator

MATERIALS:

Homemade clay:
- ½ cup salt
- ½ cup flour
- ½ cup cornstarch
- 3 T. white non-toxic glue
- water

Decoration:
- acrylic craft paint in blue, white
- paper towels

Optional:
Clear glaze

Traditional Fine Arts

STEPS:

1. Pour salt, flour and cornstarch into bowl and blend. Then add glue and knead for several minutes. To avoid the mess, you can also start your dough in a locking plastic bag to mix

2. Knead in drops of water gradually until you have the right clay texture. Work your clay for at least 5 minutes and then roll into a ball

3. Hollow the inside gently and evenly with your thumbs, building out the walls as much as possible while still holding the shape. For faster drying choose a sunny window or outdoors

4. Once dry, sketch on a design and paint the bowl. You may want to work out your design on a sheet of paper first. If you want your bowl bright white, put a white coat of paint down first and let it dry. Then sketch your design for the blue over that

Paint your design carefully with the smaller brush. Take your time and let the areas dry before painting next to them

Did You Know?

+ On true Ming pottery, the artists never put the mark or seal of their own name on the base of the piece. Instead they would put the name of the ruling emperor of the time

传统艺术

2.

3.

4.

BRUSH PAINTED SCROLL
毛笔画轴

Three Friends of Winter 岁寒三友

Chinese scroll painting is one of the oldest continuous artistic traditions in the world and dates back to the late 4th century AD with Zhejiang Province being an early birthplace. Originally painted scrolls were ornamental designs and patterns painted on silk, and as the art form evolved, they included recorded information, calligraphic messages of inspiration and many themes. Traditionally a painting includes imagery, calligraphy (poetry or something else fitting to the theme) and a chop identifying the artist.

Landscapes and other subjects from nature are the most painted, and 'Three Friends of Winter' is one common theme throughout history. The nature elements in 'Three Friends of Winter' have been planted together in Chinese gardens throughout history and depicted through art and poetic calligraphy. While many plants and trees begin to die when winter approaches, the pine, plum blossom, and bamboo do just the opposite with their survival and vitality. These three strong plants that thrive and sustain in the cold are symbolically compared to friends that can be looked to for support.

YOU'LL NEED:

- Watercolor (tube or pan)
- Black ink (or paint)
- Brushes in 3 sizes including traditional Chinese or Japanese brush, if possible
- Weights for paper corners, if necessary
- Palette or plate

MATERIALS:

- Authentic Xuan paper or other natural rice fiber paper (watercolor or printmaking rag stock if you want it heavier) cut to desired scroll dimensions
- Water in a small tub
- Paper towels

Traditional Fine Arts

传统艺术

Bamboo 竹

Strength and peace, stamina, abundance, flexibility- bends but never breaks

Plum Blossom 梅花

Symbolizes the end of winter and new growth and opportunities

Pine Tree 松树

Long life, endurance, faith, powerful (trunk) of strength

Three Friends of Winter, Ma Yuan, c. 1160-1225

SCHOLAR'S DESK

Before beginning a painting, a traditional Chinese brush painter prepares his or her work area and contemplates the expression of nature that will be painted. This often includes assembling the "four treasures of the scholar's desk"; an ink stone, ink stick, brushes and paper surface.

No matter what materials you are using, take a few minutes to set up your area, relax, check your good posture and think about the painting you are about to create.

BRUSH PAINTED SCROLL

毛笔画轴

PAINTING TECHNIQUES GUIDE

1. Marks and Strokes- Practice the push and pull, dots and lines, washes and shapes that can be created with different sizes of brushes before painting on the scroll. Try and express a smooth flow of energy and beauty with every stroke

2. Try 2 or more colors on the same brush to get a varied stroke (similar to how colors blend and reflect in nature)

3. Paint from lightest to darkest

4. Paint from largest washes to smallest detail

STEPS:

1. Sketch your design lightly in pencil. Try to compose a pleasing arrangement of the three elements bamboo, pine and plum blossom to fill the strong vertical shape. Use natural or photo reference if possible

2. Prepare your paint and ink by blending and diluting the colors you will need for your subjects on a palette or plate- remember your black ink or paint can dilute to many shades of gray

3. Follow the Painting Techniques Guide to begin- first with your background washes

4. Allow areas to dry that you plan to overpaint or add detail unless the bleeded wet color is what you desire- take your time

5. Add your signature or seal (see lesson on chop p. 18)

GRAIN OF RICE

This lesson is just a brief overview of a very complex historic art form that takes years to master. Think of ways to simplify the lesson for younger artists such as choosing one simple subject that includes 2 or 3 strokes and limited colors

✱ See Additional Resources and Information on p. 136 for supply retailers

Upright

45-degree

Horizontal

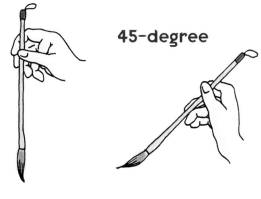

侍统艺术

Brush Positions

These three common positions for holding the brush are used for different stroke styles. The traditional stroke is painted in one flowing move, so having the loaded brush in the best position before it touches the painting surface allows the most control. (In contrast, in Western painting artists often sketch their image first and then go back and rework areas.) These positions also allow the artist to be the most expressive and creative with each paint mark.

Constructing your hanging scroll:

1. Cut dowels or bamboo to extend 2″ beyond width of scroll

2. Curl top and bottom around dowel (so sticks are on back) leaving ½″ extra

3. Secure with glue, tape or hand stitching

4. Tie cord to each end of top stick to hang

ALSO TRY

Traditional Papermaking p. 20

Calligraphy Strokes p. 10

Chop Art p 18

CHOP ART 印章

The Chinese chop or seal is a carved stamp used to sign documents and personalize artwork. Chops were used historically in the Shang Dynasty (1523-1028 B.C.) by Chinese nobility and officials to place their personal mark. One of the earliest treasured seals was made for the First Emperor of China, Qin Shihuang from a precious jade stone.

As time went on, using a chop or seal became an essential business practice for banking or exchanging goods. Even today in China, most documents and contracts are not valid without a personal, business or government stamp from the seals of the people involved.

Another important use of the chop or seal is as a personal "signature" on paintings and calligraphy works. The red seal imprint enhances the composition of a painting or calligraphy piece as a part of the artwork.

Chops are made of many materials, such as metal, stone, wood, and jade and the characters on them can be carved in many styles. Both the chop and its stamp are carefully designed and are considered works of art whether simple or ornate. Each one is unique which adds value to new finely crafted chops, and interest in older rare collectible pieces.

Here you can choose a character from the calligraphy guide or create your own design. The traditional red ink for stamping is often cinnabar paste but a basic red ink pad will work just fine with your seal as you leave your own "mark" on your special papers and artwork!

YOU'LL NEED:

MATERIALS:

• Tracing paper

• Craft foam white sheet

• Corrugated cardboard 3" x 14" (with ridge pattern horizontal for easy folding)

• Red stamp pad and paper

• Craft paint and brush (optional)

GRAIN OF RICE

Decorate the top end of your chop with a print of your design on white board trimmed neatly and taped, or glue on a small flat bottomed trinket, animal or toy

✳ See p. 129 for more character ideas for your chop

STEPS:

1. Draw your character or design in dark pencil on tracing paper to fit a 1 ¼" square; then flip it over and trace it in reverse on to the foam sheet. The pencil graphite will leave a line and small indent

2. Remove tracing paper and retrace with a ball point pen, pressing down to leave smooth, thick grooves for stamping

3. Cut the foam to a 1 ¼" square with the design centered, then cut a second 1 ¼" square for an extra layer

4. Fold cardboard in a spiral, creasing flat sides as it gets larger so it makes a long cubic shape

5. When folded, tape closed securely along long edge. Paint if desired

6. Glue two layers of foam on one end with design facing out

Did You Know?

+ A Chinese chop carved out of stone and dipped in red ink is thought to mean your paperwork or contract is "set in stone" and "signed in blood" when stamped

1.    **2.**    **3.**

4.    **5.**    **6.**

This is the character for "love"

ALSO TRY

Brush Painted Scroll p. 14

Calligraphy Strokes p. 10

TRADITIONAL PAPERMAKING 传统造纸

One of China's oldest inventions is paper. The first papermaking method was invented in about 105 A.D. by Ts'ai Lun, an official at the Chinese Imperial Court during the Han Dynasty (206 B.C. to 220 A.D.) although a few earlier paper scraps have been discovered in recent years. It is recorded that Ts'ai Lun presented Emperor Han Ho Ti with his first paper samples. They were made by pounding mulberry tree bark or other natural plant fibers with a wooden mallet to break them down to pulp.

Ts'ai Lun 蔡伦

The papermaking industry in China grew rapidly and paper soon replaced silk as the common material for scholars, poets and artists and many other useful purposes. It is fun and easy to make your own sheets of handmade paper which can be used for everything from calligraphy and artwork to gifts and handmade books.

YOU'LL NEED:

• Mould and deckle frame (see steps)

• Kitchen blender (use with adult)

• Wooden spoon

• Plastic bucket

• Plastic container or cup

• Heavy-duty stapler or duct tape

• Deep, large plastic tray or bin for submerging mould and deckle into pulp

MATERIALS:

• Scrap paper (high fiber/low quality is best and remember colored paper will tint pulp)

• Water

• Thick newspaper pads or felt for blotting moisture

• 2 identical basic wooden picture frames (size that you want largest paper sheets)

• Screen at least 1" larger than frame on all sides; use window screen or plastic mesh

GRAIN OF RICE

Be creative and add dried flowers, food color, grasses, colored thread, glitter or anything that you can stir into the pulp to add your personal touch

1.

2.

3.

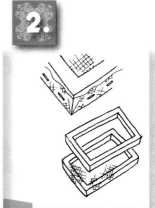

Traditional Fine Arts

STEPS:

1. Rip paper into small pieces and put in bucket. Add 3 parts water and let soak for at least an hour

2. Take one frame and stretch screen or mesh over flat back side. Attach securely around side edges with staples or duct tape as this will be your mould. The deckle frame stays open and rests on top

3. Pour soaked paper into blender in batches and blend covered on low; pour the slurry into the large tray (should be larger than frames)

4. Hold frames together firmly with the mould on the bottom and screen surface on the inside and lower into slurry, allowing the pulp to settle in the top deckle frame. Then gently lift out, let drain and remove deckle. Flip the mould frame quickly on a bed of newspaper or felt surface

5. Dab the screen side with a sponge to help flatten paper sheet and pull moisture out

6. Gently lift off frame and allow paper to dry. Move sheet to a dryer surface or speed up the process with a blow dryer or warm sun if desired

Did You Know?

+ Before the Chinese used raw tree and plant fibers for paper, they used anything they had that could be pounded into pulp including clothing, rags and fishing nets

SCRAPS- All kinds of paper can be soaked and blended into your slurry- a great way to recycle

ALSO TRY

Calligraphy Strokes p. 10

PAPERMAKING TERMS

Mould and deckle - Set of frames used to screen and press handmade paper

Pulp - Broken down cell walls of fibrous plants such as wood, cotton, or hemp used to make paper

Slurry - A liquid mixture of water and fiber pulp used to make paper

Sieve - Screened surface attached to mould for separating pulp from moisture

PAPERCUT DESIGNS
剪纸

Paper cutting has been an important and respected folk art in China for nearly 2000 years. Generations still pass down the artistry and skill of making papercuts for birthday and wedding celebrations, festivals, gifts and home. The designs are used to decorate gates, doors and walls to bring good luck.

Traditional papercuts often illustrate natural subjects, scenes and stories of daily life and the zodiac symbols. Many designs and patterns are also used for embroidery guides. The papercut styles and subjects are different all around China as some are more graphic and fun while others are very intricate and delicate in design and detail.

These two designs are traditional themes but have been adapted so that they can be cut with scissors instead of an engraver's knife, which is another method many Chinese use. Here you also use a fold and cut "snowflake" technique instead of needing to poke through the design to cut out areas.

YOU'LL NEED:

MATERIALS:

- Lightweight 8 ½ x 11" paper (red is traditional) or other solid, patterned or metallic stock
- Mounting paper 8 ½ x 11" (optional)

 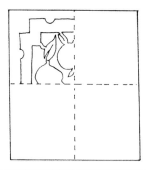

Templates before folding

The **'peach'** design represents longevity, immortality, and is thought to ward off evil. It is auspicious to give as a "long life" birthday gift at family celebrations

GRAIN OF RICE

If you happen to make an error and cut through an area not marked you have two choices: when done, glue and mount the design and the slice will disappear OR take a new sheet and start over until you get it right!

Traditional Fine Arts

The **'double fish'** is symbolic for abundance and wealth. Cut in red, it is even more lucky. One tradition is to hang it in the kitchen to attract plenty of food and provisions for the family

Did You Know?

+ In rural peasant villages paper-cuts are displayed to decorate the inside windows of homes which often have paper panes. In the evening with the lantern's glow inside, they can also be seen as shadow designs from outdoors

传统艺术

STEPS:

1. Copy or trace design from templates on pp. 109 & 110

2. Follow diagram fold instructions on dotted lines for design selected (If helpful, tack edges closed with small pieces of tape after folding to make cutting more precise on all the layers)

3. Carefully snip away areas marked, neatly following the solid lines, then gently open and smooth creases

4. Flip over so guide lines don't appear and mount onto background paper if desired

1.

2.

3.

4.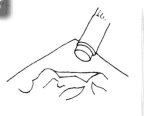

ALSO TRY

Celebration Garland p. 34

Shadow Puppets p. 76

KNOT TYING 传统中国结

The Chinese decorative knot comes from the ancient folk art of tying beautiful and auspicious knot designs made of colorful silk thread. This handcraft dates back to Zhou Dynasty, developed further in the T'ang and Song Dynasties, and was popularized in Ming and Qing Dynasties. Specific knots are used to express good wishes including happiness, prosperity, love and the absence of evil.

Crafting the Chinese knot is a three-step process which involves tying a knot from a single rope, tightening it, and adding any decorative finishing touches. Knot tying methods are standard, but the tightening can determine the degree of tension in a knot, the length of loops (ears) and the smoothness and orderliness of the lines. How well a Chinese knot has been tightened can demonstrate the skill and artistry of the knot artist. "Finishing" a knot can include inlaying pearls, beads or other precious stones, starching the knot into certain patterns, or simply gently tugging, adjusting and smoothing the knot until it's perfect.

YOU'LL NEED:

MATERIALS:
- Silk or cotton cord or thin rope approx. 24 "
- Small square of paper

Optional:
- Small sheet cork, foamcore or corrugated cardboard for mounting the knot cord if desired
- Common pins
(see Grain of Rice)

GRAIN OF RICE

Another classic way to construct your knot is to secure the loops on foam core, cork or corrugated cardboard with common pins as you do the steps

The **Good Luck Knot** shown here is traditionally kept or given away as a lucky token. The paper template is one method of keeping the ropes controlled and requires less tangled fingers, but some use nothing at all, or a pin board for the tying process.

Traditional Fine Arts

传统艺术

STEPS:

1. Cut cord to length and tape ends to prevent fraying and make looping easier (like a shoelace tip)

2. Take small paper square and punch 4 holes to create your template. Pull top loop through and then side loops (bights) and then the 2 loose ends together through the bottom making sure 3 loops are even in size

3. Tie loops as shown step by step on next page, in a counter-clockwise direction (a.-d.) and then clockwise direction (e.-h.). As you do each step keep control of the loops and pull them gently until snug

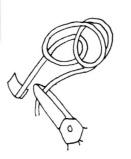

March,1520, Tang Yin,
Blowing a Bamboo Flute

back

First crowned layer from steps a.-d. on p. 26

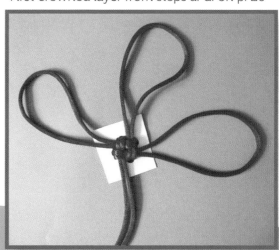

STEPS a-d

a. Fold the top bight down over the left bight

b. Fold the left bight over what was the top bight and the bottom bight

c. Fold the bottom bight over what was the left bight and the right bight

d. Fold the right bight over what was the bottom bight and under the top bight near the holes in the template. You are done with the first set of steps and have crowned the bottom layer of the knot (see photo on p. 25).

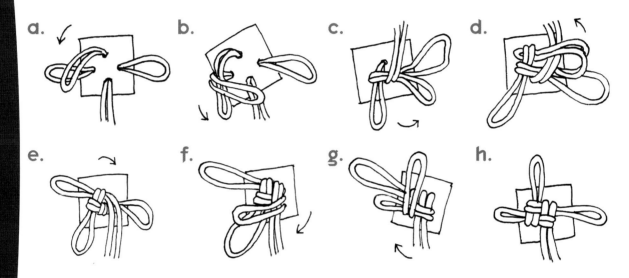

(see photo on p. 25)

TYING TIPS:

• Some cords are easier than others to tie and tighten; if you choose something too thick or too "slippery" it will be more difficult to tighten the knot. Experiment with different types of cord

• Watch that the loops stay aligned correctly and flat as you tie so the two sides of the loop don't criss-cross, or get tightened unevenly

• Be patient! Like most traditional Chinese arts, knot tying is a tricky skill that takes practice; as you try it a few times and start remembering the steps it will get much easier. Before you know it you will move on to the many wonderful different styles of more complex Chinese knots

Traditional Fine Arts

In the first layer, you did a counterclockwise crown; you are now beginning to do a clockwise crown for the top layer.

STEPS e-h

e. Fold the top bight down over the right bight

f. Fold the right bight over what was the top bight and the bottom bight

g. Fold the bottom bight over what was the right bight and the left bight

h. Fold the left bight over what was the bottom bight and under the top to finish the tying and then gently tighten

Did You Know?

✦ In China there are strict rules on where to hang or how to use Chinese knots depending on the style and custom. For instance the "blessing knot" is hung mostly on the walls in a home, as it symbolizes a festivity and atmosphere, while others might be placed on a doorknob, in a car, or used to adorn clothing, lamps or other belongings

传统艺术

Finished "Good Luck' knot

STEPS:

4. Before tearing off the paper template flip it over; you can adjust the small loops (ears) by tugging on them evenly to the size you want on the finished knot, being careful to keep the cord aligned properly and not pulling out any of the loops

5. Rip off the paper template and do any small adjustments and tightening

Festivals & Holidays

节日和假日

FESTiVALS
& HOLiDAYS

ABOUT CHINESE FESTIVALS

The uniqueness of China is perhaps most celebrated during traditional festivals and holidays throughout the lunar year. Each has a rich history and customs that have survived many dynasties and the essence of these festivals is still strong, with some modern twists. The family is at the heart of these celebrations, which revolve around events and parades, special meals and treats, and spiritual offerings.

Spring Festival 春节

(Also called Chinese or Lunar New Year)

This is by far the most important holiday in China, and marks the beginning of the lunar calendar from the first day to the 15th, in late January or February. The Chinese use a lunar calendar based on the moon cycles following a long history of rural agriculture planting and harvesting seasons.

Preparations are made long before the first eve and people travel great distances to return to their provinces and towns and share their time off while businesses are closed. They visit with relatives, friends and neighbors while they honor gods and family ancestors. The streets are alive with lights, noise, parades and lion dances.

New Year Customs:

- Clean to sweep away bad luck before the holiday

- Pay off debts to start fresh

- Hang red decorations with auspicious symbols

- Wear new clothing and shoes

- Put away knives and scissors

- Make peace and show kindness to family and friends

- Honor the Kitchen God with a picture or sacrifice

- Pay visits with gifts and money envelopes

ORANGES AND TANGERINES (Ji)– **good luck, wealth**
WHOLE FISH (Yu)– **abundance**
NOODLE (long, uncut)– **long life**
WHOLE CHICKEN (best with head and feet)– **family unity**
CAKE (Nian gao)– **improve or get higher**
TRAY OF TOGETHERNESS TREATS– **"sweet" year**
DUMPLINGS (Jiaozi)– **prosperity, luck**

Lantern Festival 元宵节

At the end of the Spring Festival on the 15th day, the Lantern Festival is celebrated for three days. People gather in the streets and raise lanterns to the night sky to try and see their departed loved ones passing over on their journey to the heavens. Even in modern China you will find millions of lanterns strung across streets in cities and towns as well as around homes as symbols of good fortune while the children enjoy glutinous sweet rice balls (tang yuan).

New Year FOODS

The family meal is a central part of the celebration, especially on lunar New Year's Eve. These are traditional foods served that have special meaning or similar sounds to auspicious words, although sometimes on just the first day, meat and fish are not served.

Dragon Boat Festival 端午节

On the 5th day of the 5th lunar month, the Dragon Boat Festival or Duan Wu is celebrated. It honors the great poet Qu Yuan from the 3rd century B.C., a top advisor to the Chu kingdom that lost his life in the Milo River as a sacrifice on that day. Dragon boat racing is the main event with beautifully crafted dragon boats holding large crews of paddlers. Glutinous rice dumplings (zongzi) wrapped in bamboo leaves with many fillings are a symbolic snack that is always enjoyed on this day. Children also wear incense pouches to ward off evil spirits.

Other Traditional Holidays

- Tomb Sweeping Day (Qingming) 12th day of the 3rd lunar month

- National Day (People's Republic of China anniversary) October 1st

- Winter Solstice Festival (Dongzhi) in December on shortest day, longest night

Mid-Autumn Moon Festival 中秋节

This end of harvest festival falls on the 15th day of 8th lunar month. People gather outdoors to view the auspicious fullest moon to be in harmony with nature and share legends of the mythical Moon Goddess of Immortality. It is also known as the Moon Cake Festival because it is a time to gather with family, share good food and offer moon cakes, a special pastry filled with bean paste.

NEW YEAR "FU" BANNER

新年福字

"Fu" has always been the most important Chinese character shared during the Spring Festival. It means good fortune, happiness and blessings. It is displayed on doors and other places of celebration as an important good wish, and is often combined with other auspicious new year images and symbols in decorations (see the Auspicious Chinese Symbols guide on p.130).

Throughout history calligraphers have been writing this character artistically on red paper to display with red couplets, hanging lanterns and other festive decorations. This banner is simple yet perfect for displaying in your home during Chinese New Year, or to make as an offering to someone special during this important season of family and friends.

YOU'LL NEED:

• use white glue
• brush is for glue

MATERIALS:

• Red construction paper 9"x12"
• White bond copy paper 8 1/2 " x 11"
• Gold glitter

STEPS:

1. Cut red paper to a 9" square

2. Copy template on p. 124 on to white paper

3. Cut out Fu panel carefully around edges

4. Spread glue neatly inside lines of Fu character and border decorations

5. Sprinkle generously with glitter and shake off excess into box lid to reuse

6. After drying, glue and mount the Fu panel in the center of the red square

GRAIN OF RICE

If you are working slowly with small children to apply the glue and glitter, do a section at a time so the glue doesn't dry too quickly

Festivals & Holidays

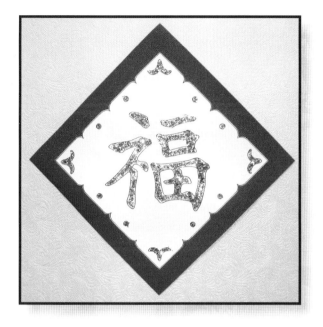

Did You Know?

✦ A similar sound of Fu with a different inflection means "bat". As a result, bats are symbolic for bringing good fortune and they bring even more blessings if five bats (wu-fu) are in the design

"Fu" is often displayed upside-down on the front door of a home to signify that good luck has arrived. The upside-down character sounds the same as the character for "luck comes"

ALSO TRY

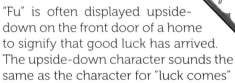

Papercut Designs
p. 22

Spring Couplets
p. 40

CELEBRATION GARLAND
拉花

Festive paper garlands are often used in China as decorations for holidays and celebrations. They've become popular in recent years starting around the 1970's when manufacturing made them widely available and inexpensive. Although they are modern, you can recognize other influences such as traditional papercuts and origami in this craft.

These colorful garlands are displayed to symbolize happiness and joy. When big holidays or family celebrations such as weddings or birthdays are coming, Chinese people will buy or make paper garlands for the specific theme or occasion and hang them on the wall or ceiling to decorate the event space. They can be in many different shapes such as flowers, Chinese characters and silhouettes of objects, or have a simpler ornamental design.

Assembling your garland requires a little patience but is not difficult. Although they are sold in some party shops imported from China, here you can be creative and make your own! You can "go green" by using extra scraps of tissue paper you have on hand, and you will be impressed at how beautiful your handmade garland turns out compared to something purchased.

YOU'LL NEED:

MATERIALS:

- Tissue paper in assorted colors
- Strong thread and needle (sharp, use caution!)

STEPS:

1. Draw 5 ½" diameter circles on tissue paper. Tracing a small bowl or plate works well

2. Cut out circles in equal quantities of each color. About 60 circles will make a 5-6 ft. garland

3. Fold each circle in quarters and follow the template on p. 111 for the cuts. You can copy the template and cut using it as a guide, or trace the shapes directly on to the tissue paper

4. Snip out the patterns and open and flatten the pieces. You can stack, fold and cut a few at a time but do so neatly because they should match perfectly

GRAIN OF RICE

Try different shapes, cutouts and tissue papers to decorate for your own Chinese festival or special event. Also try folded accordion style for a simple no-glue method

节日和假日

5. Match up and glue two together on four corners, then glue on the next one, but just in the middle. Continue this alternating glue pattern making sure you end on four corners

6. Once all glued, gently push the threaded needle through the stack center. Thread all the way through to the other end, leaving several inches of extra thread on each side

7. Hang your garland against a wall or across a doorway or room. The thread keeps it stable along with having ends to attach for hanging. It also makes it easy to retract for safekeeping when you take it down

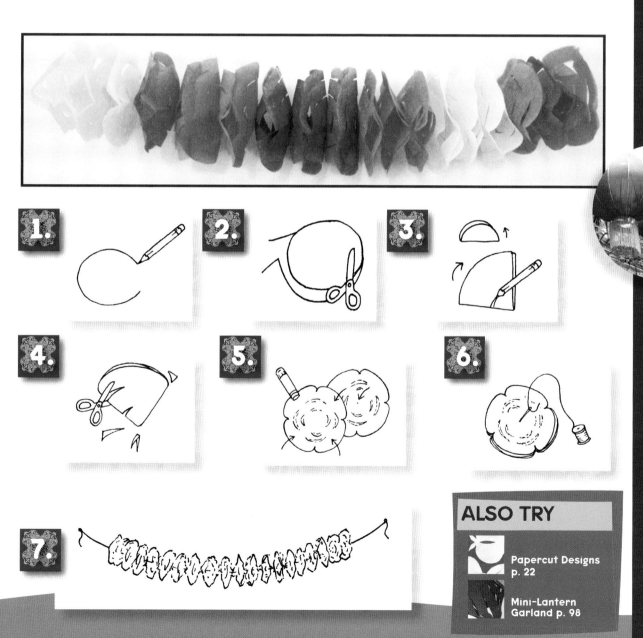

ALSO TRY

Papercut Designs p. 22

Mini-Lantern Garland p. 98

DRAGON PARADE COSTUME
舞龙的道具服饰

The Dragon Dance is a famous, exciting cultural event and the highlight of most Chinese New Year parades. This traditional dance, alive with movement, color and the noise of drums and firecrackers is also performed at other important events, holiday festivals and at the opening of new businesses.

It began during the Han Dynasty (206 B.C.-220 A.D.) and became popular during the Tang (618 A.D.-906 A.D.) and Song (960-1279 A.D.) Dynasties. In early history, people performed a dragon dance when they worshipped gods for favorable weather for agriculture and to heal sickness. Gradually dragon dances also became an important way to attract luck and celebrate new life at Chinese New Year.

The classic dragon costume consists of the dragon head mask carried by the leader, ornately painted in customary colors of red, green, and gold and a long sectional covered bamboo frame held up by the rest of the strong dancers. Sometimes the mask is rigged with pulleys to animate the mouth and tongue, and the most elaborate ones have pyrotechnic devices that emit real smoke and sparks to simulate the fiery breath of the dragon.

This simpler version is a great project to do with a group. You can brainstorm together about how to make the structure, features and decorations.

YOU'LL NEED:

• Glue gun works best- always use with adult supervision
• Utility knife (optional and only with adult supervision)

MATERIALS:

• 2 cardboard cartons (17 ½" x 11 ¼" x 8 ¾") with lids

• 1 gift wrap or shipping cardboard tube (30")

• 3 styrofoam balls (2) 4" diam. and (1) 3" diam. (halved)

• Colored paper, paint or material to cover head

• Festive fabric for body approx. 60" wide and 1 yd. per dancer plus 1 yd. for the tail end

• Colored craft foam and decorating materials

GRAIN OF RICE

If the mouth flap gets too droopy, punch holes in the sides and make a hinge out of a thick elastic cut open and tied, or brass fastener attaching the top to bottom. The mouth will be partially open and still move.

STEPS: (step drawings- p.38)

1. Review diagrams on p. 127. Cut 2" off the top edge of one of the boxes

2. Cut sides of the lid at 10", gently crease the back surface; this will be the hinged mouth

3. Cover over the entire outer surface of both boxes and lid with solid colored paint, or adhere paper or fabric

4. Connect largest box to smaller one so bottoms are flush (both upside-down with lid placed back on smaller box) with glue gun and/or heavy tape. The smaller box should be sticking out the long way for the nose and mouth

5. Draw and cut out features from craft foam, cardboard or other materials (see Shapes for Head Decoration) and adhere with glue gun. Remember to make two of each where needed! Sides of nose are styrofoam ball halves painted and eyeballs are white larger balls with foam details as illustrated on p. 126

6. Cut hole in back bottom area of smaller box where it is not flapped down, just big enough to insert tube snugly for handle. Put glue on tube end, insert tube and secure with glue gun around opening. Reinforce once dry by covering glued seam with tape

7. Attach the fabric end along the inside back three sides with glue gun. You can reinforce with staples or other materials if necessary

MAKING THE HEAD

The head is the focus of the costume and expresses the personality and excitement leading off the dance or parade. This design can be made in one session with the two boxes and readily available materials. Add your decorations and features and then step back to be sure your dragon looks dramatic from a distance.

If you have more time and skill you can make the head as elaborate as you want. Some people use paper mache built up on the box base or over a wire armature to get a more detailed form. You can also do an original design from flat cardboard if you want to customize the shape or size. If you plan to use it at a major event or for several years, you will want to make it as sturdy and professional looking as possible. You can also use fabric in place of paper or foam on the surface of the head, for streamers, or for other decorations.

ALSO TRY

Ribbon Dance Stick p. 64

Lion Dance Mask p. 70

DRAGON PARADE COSTUME
舞龙的道具服饰 CONTINUED

1.

2.

3.

4.

5.

6.

7.

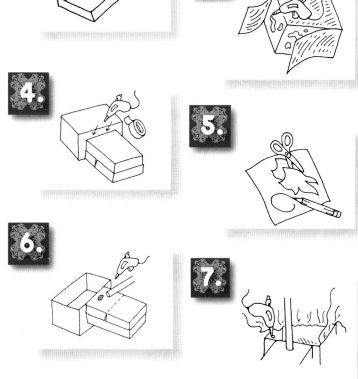

See diagrams on p. 127

TIPS FOR DECORATING

• Decorate the head and body with materials such as glitter pens, felt, sequins, glitter pom-poms, shiny cord or trims, fabric markers and metallic paint. Keep in mind the large scale of this craft; you'll need to go big on everything you add

• The body cloth can be edged with fringe, pom-poms, wide ribbon or anything you have on hand. You can also cut the fabric edge with a zig-zag pattern of "scale" points

• You can make the eyes "glow" by gluing on gold or translucent white glitter

• Cut point shapes on ends of hanging wide ribbon or streamers

• For a long dragon you can connect several pieces of cloth to make the body if you can't get several yards in one piece

• Be sure to check the clearance table at your fabric store as this quantity of fabric can get expensive. If you are having some simple fun with the dragon costume and it isn't for a performance, any lightweight sheet can be used

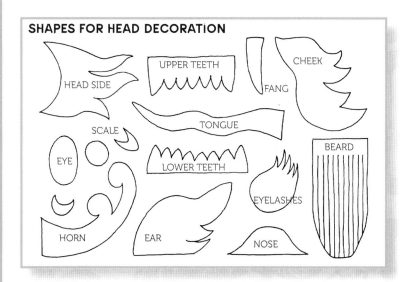

SHAPES FOR HEAD DECORATION

HEAD SIDE

UPPER TEETH

CHEEK

FANG

SCALE

TONGUE

EYE

LOWER TEETH

BEARD

EYELASHES

HORN

EAR

NOSE

Did You Know?

+ In a celebration it is believed that the longer the dragon, the more good fortune it will bring to the people and location. Some traditional performing dragons are as long as 70 meters (over 200 ft.) with more than 25 sections

DRAGONS IN CHINA:

Dragons were originally considered "the spirit of the river", and were believed to inhabit all forms of water from lakes, to puddles, to rain. Throughout history dragons have been very meaningful symbols to Chinese people who may refer to themselves as "Lung Tik Chuan Ren", Descendents of the Dragon. They are considered to be divine mythical creatures that bring lifelong abundance, prosperity and good fortune. The features embody several different animals, giving the dragon its unusual powers. People born in the Year of the Dragon are believed to receive all these good offerings and also possess intelligence, wisdom and courage.

HOW TO HAVE A DRAGON DANCE PARADE:

In a professional dance the raising and lowering of the head is followed by a long body constructed in sections supported on poles carried by the dancers. The dance mimics the flow of a river and often has impressive choreography that can take considerable training to master.

The first person holds a "Pearl of Wisdom" ball to lead the direction of the dragon. The second controls the dragon's head while the rest hold the dragon's body. Loud and rhythmic drum musicians accompany the dragon to scare away the evil spirits and add to the festive atmosphere.

For your parade you can put the dancers under the train of cloth for the dragon body but they do not need poles. Young dancers can simply hold the edges of the cloth or hold on to the waist or shoulders of the child in front of them. Dancers can wear similar colored clothing or matching Chinese brocade outfits. The leader holding the head can have fringe or ribbon streamers attached to their costume to stand out.

Practice as a group in a large space before your event. Determine your route and try and swerve the dancers back and forth behind the animated movements of the head like a long, flowing water dragon.

SPRING COUPLETS 春联

The Spring Couplet (or Chun lian) is displayed during the Chinese New Year around the doorway entrance or offered as a gift. It is two vertical strips of red paper mounted on each side of the door and one horizontal strip across the top. There are many different stories of the first couplets from the Five Dynasties period in North China (between the Tang and Song Dynasties) which then were "door gods" engraved on peach wood planks. Over time, the tradition changed to ink calligraphy on red paper to ward off evil spirits.

The most important idea about the couplet is the positive message or poem about spring renewal and good wishes that is written in your best calligraphy. The greeting or poem will differ depending on who is creating it and where it will be displayed, but the left and right panels must have the same character counts on each side, same structure and same harmony in spoken sound.

You can try this couplet freehand, sketching in pencil first and then using marker or ink from the character reference to make it more authentic, but tracing, copying or transferring it is much easier if you are new to Chinese characters!

YOU'LL NEED:

MATERIALS:

• Red construction paper 12x18", two sheets (if you only have smaller paper, it can be taped together to make the same size)

• Tracing paper

STEPS:

1. Cut and tape red paper to make 3 pieces; two at 6" x 24" and one at 6" x 12"

2. Copy couplet calligraphy on p. 125 at 200%

3. Trace the outline of the characters neatly with pencil for the two long vertical lines and one short horizontal line; you can do them in position or on separate squares

4. Color characters in with black marker pen

5. Trim tracing paper into neat squares around characters if separate

6. Position the tracing paper calligraphy characters evenly on the three red panels to make your couplet. Then glue them down as smoothly as possible so the red paper shows through

GRAIN OF RICE

"Brush pen" black markers, found in most craft stores can give an authentic calligraphy style. You can also use a metallic gold pen to outline the characters

Festivals & Holidays

节日和假日

HERE iS A GOOD MESSAGE FOR YOUR COUPLET AND THE TRANSLATION iN CHiNESE:

- Families and friends get together to welcome a new year happily 欢聚一堂迎新年
  First sentence (Shanglian) which is the right, vertical top to bottom
- Full of laughter and happiness is how people celebrate the new year 欢声笑语贺新春
  Second sentence (Xialian) which is the left, vertical top to bottom
- The whole family is and will be happy in the new year 合家欢乐
  Shorter sentence (Hengpi) or words along the top, left to right

 **1.**

 **2.**

 **3.**

 **4.**

 **5.**

6.

合家欢乐

欢声笑语贺新春

欢聚一堂迎新年

ALSO TRY

New Year "Fu" Banner p. 32

Calligraphy Strokes p. 10

Papercut Designs p. 22

LUCKY RED ENVELOPE
压岁钱或红包

Giving lucky money (hong bao or lai see) is a Chinese traditional custom. When the lunar new year is coming and especially on New Year's Eve, elder generations always give lucky money to young children expressing their best wishes to them. Symbols of wealth and luck are often on the outside.

For elder generations, this custom means that the money will bring good luck (and good fortune) to their children or grandchildren. For younger generations, after they receive the money, usually they will put it under their pillows or in the pockets of their new year's clothing. The lucky money is put in a red envelope because red in China represents good luck. Red envelopes are also presented to adults on social and family occasions such as birthdays and wedding receptions.

YOU'LL NEED:

MATERIALS:
• Red bond paper 8 ½ x 11"

Chinese 'Fu' character on envelope means "good fortune" or "good luck"

GRAIN OF RICE

If you don't have red bond paper or a copy machine, you can trace the envelope template contour on to any paper and add color, art, calligraphy or rubber stamps

 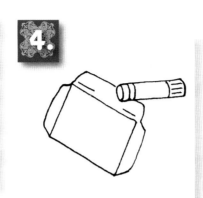

Did You Know?

✦ The amount of money in the envelope is usually even, not odd which is considered unlucky except avoid four... it represents death! Eight is especially auspicious

STEPS:

1. Copy template on p. 112 on to red bond paper (you can reduce size and do 2 per page if necessary)

2. Cut out contour of envelope

3. Fold crease at center and flap dotted lines with design on the outside

4. Fold in panel and glue down side flap, then bottom flap to form envelope. Don't forget to leave top flap open for gift money before sealing!

CUSTOMS FOR RED ENVELOPE

- Use crisp new bills when giving money
- Offer with both hands
- Receive with gratitude and don't open in front of giver
- Young children are usually given less money than older children and teens

ZODIAC ANIMALS 十二生肖

The Chinese zodiac is identified by twelve specific animals for the cycle of lunar years. This is celebrated at Chinese New Year and also characterizes a person's birth year and their personality traits. In China people often refer to their animal year of birth instead of their actual birthday. Each year is also attached to one of the five elements; wood, fire, earth, metal or water.

The zodiac animal lunar cycle is also so influential in China that people open businesses, plan events such as weddings and make important life decisions based on the best timing of the animal year calendar. This decoration can be made for any year and is perfect to hang during Spring Festival or give as a gift to someone born under that animal.

YOU'LL NEED:

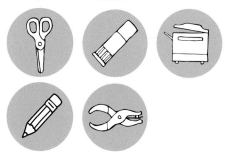

MATERIALS:

• Red bond, construction paper or cover weight paper

• Gold or patterned paper

• White copy paper

• Plastic pony beads

• Ribbon, cord, yarn or thick thread (about 8") for hanging

• Thick thread, embroidery floss or thin yarn for tassel

STEPS:

1. Copy the animal and Chinese character on p. 126 that represents the year you are celebrating

2. Cut out a circle around the animal or cut and glue it on to a white circle (you can trace a lid or cup)

3. Trace large octagon on to red paper and small octagon on to gold or patterned paper (template on p. 111); cut them both out

4. Glue together the large and small octagons and then the circle design on top

GRAIN OF RICE

You can mount the paper shape on to stiff board or foamboard and trim for a more sturdy decoration or gift

STORY OF THE ZODIAC ANIMALS

According to Chinese folklore Buddha (or the Jade Emperor) invited all the animals on earth for a New Year celebration, but only twelve appeared. To reward those animals, Buddha named a year after each of them in the order that they crossed the river, starting with the Rat that arrived by riding on the Ox's back and then cleverly jumped off to win the race. That placed the Ox second, then the strong Tiger, jumping Rabbit, Dragon, Snake, Horse, Goat, Monkey, Rooster, Dog and finally the slow, happy Pig.

* See p. 133 in the Project Resources section for more ideas for zodiac animal crafts

Festivals & Holidays

5. Punch holes in the top and bottom

6. Thread a bead on to the hanging cord and tie a loop from the top hole

7. Make tassel by cutting several pieces of 6" thread, fold in half, tie together, and then coil a small piece around the top

8. Thread and tie another small piece through top of tassel, thread on beads and tie to bottom hole

1.

2.

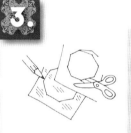

3.

4.

5.

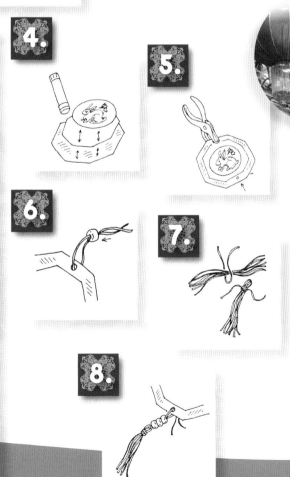

BiRTH YEAR ANiMALS AND TRAiTS

RAT: 1936, 1948, 1960, 1972, 1984, 1996, 2008, 2020
Charming, Adventurous, Ambitious

OX: 1925, 1937, 1949, 1961, 1973, 1985, 1997, 2009
Patient, Hardworking, Trustworthy

TiGER: 1926, 1938, 1950, 1962, 1974, 1986, 1998, 2010
Powerful, Protective, Rebellious

RABBiT: 1927, 1939, 1951, 1963, 1975, 1987, 1999, 2011
Lucky, Affectionate , Peaceful

DRAGON: 1928, 1940, 1952, 1964, 1976, 1988, 2000, 2012
Strong, Powerful, Wise

SNAKE: 1929, 1941, 1953, 1965, 1977, 1989, 2001, 2013
Determined, Intense, Beautiful

HORSE: 1930, 1942, 1954, 1966, 1978, 1990, 2002, 2014
Attractive, Talkative, Restless

GOAT: 1931, 1943, 1955, 1967, 1979, 1991, 2003, 2015
Elegant, Creative, Sympathetic

MONKEY: 1932, 1944, 1956, 1968, 1980, 1992, 2004, 2016
Charming, Inventive, Successful

ROOSTER: 1933, 1945, 1957, 1969, 1981, 1993, 2005, 2017
Proud, Confident, Inquisitive

DOG: 1934, 1946, 1958, 1970, 1982, 1994, 2006, 2018
Loyal, Sincere, Cooperative

PiG: 1935, 1947, 1959, 1971, 1983, 1995, 2007, 2019
Friendly, Noble, Brave

6.

7.

8.

节日和假日

FIRECRACKER FAVOR 爆竹

During Chinese New Year there has always been a great tradition of setting off loud and brilliant fireworks to ward off the ferocious monster Nian and to welcome in the Lunar New Year. The production of gunpowder (for military use) during the T'ang Dynasty (618 A.D.-906 A.D.) was eventually adapted for making fireworks when metal powders and plant fibers were added to the explosive mix for brilliant color.

The popularity and tradition of fireworks is still so strong in China that to this day they produce, use and export more fireworks than any other country in the world! You can make your own less noisy and much safer Chinese firecrackers with this craft idea. Then act out the Legend of the Nian Monster with your "firecrackers"!

YOU'LL NEED:

MATERIALS:

• Chenille stem (white or black) or Yarn
• Bath tissue cardboard tube (or paper towel tube cut in sections)
• Red tissue paper
• Gold glitter
• Filling if desired- see Grain of Rice

STEPS:

1. Cut red tissue to size 8" x approx. 16"

2. Roll the paper around the tube leaving an even amount at each end and tape or glue it securely along the side

GRAIN OF RICE

You can use the tube for stuffing candy or small toys for celebration favors before twisting closed. You can also put a handful of dried beans or rice inside to create a "firecracker noise" shaker

Festivals & Holidays

节日和假日

3. Fold in one end of tissue for the base and tape

4. Twist the other end and wrap with chenille stem for the "wick" (don't forget to add treats or noise shakers before closing)

5. Drizzle glue on and sprinkle with glitter for some sparkly sparks; you can decorate with Chinese characters or designs before applying glitter if you wish

Did You Know?

+ Even before gunpowder was discovered, the earliest "natural" firecracker explosions were made by throwing bamboo stalks into the fire. The air pockets in the fast-growing bamboo would spark and bang to ward off evil spirits!

 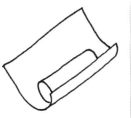 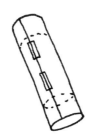 

LEGEND OF THE NiAN MONSTER 年的故事

The ancient dreaded Nian was an ugly and ferocious horned monster that would come down to the village to eat people on the cold, moonless eve of Chinese New Year. Everyone would lock their doors before sunset or run away and hide to prepare.

An old man appeared in the village with a solution and asked for the cooperation of the townspeople. They made all kinds of loud noises including drums, gongs and fireworks and lit fires to threaten and overcome the beast. They also displayed red banners to protect their homes which the monster feared. The evil Nian was conquered and the whole village celebrated!

CHOPSTICK CASES 筷子盒

THREE STYLES

Chopsticks are an essential part of Chinese food culture dating back to the Shang Dynasty (1766-1122 BCE). They are always found at Chinese festivals and holidays where there is bound to be something good to eat. Over history different materials have been used to make chopsticks including bronze, ivory, wood, bamboo and even silver and gold.

These two origami case styles have Japanese and other Asian influences but are also Chinese since paper invention led to paper functional arts. The dragon case is a simple non-traditional design craft.

You can set your table with these covers with chopstick pairs inserted or offer them as small gifts. The style 2 can even be tucked inside a card or lucky money envelope. Now you can always have your chopsticks look beautiful and stay clean until banquet time!

YOU'LL NEED: Style 3

• Optional- decoration materials for corner

MATERIALS:

• Origami or thin decorative paper from 4 5/8" (small) to 8" (large) square (style 1) and rectangle (half sheet- 6"x3" works well) (style 2)

• White cover weight stock for copying (style 3)

• Chopsticks to place inside

WHILE YOU LEARN

Here is a simple way to adapt restaurant-style chopsticks to use with less skill:

1. Break the sticks apart if attached
2. Roll a small folded piece of paper into a tight coil (chopstick wrapper works well)
3. Position it between the tops of the sticks
4. Wrap a thin rubber band to secure the top multiple times, then loop below the paper coil to hold it in place.

The chopsticks should be in a "V" shape so you can pick up food by squeezing on the tension between them

Festivals & Holidays

STYLE 1

STEPS:

1. Fold in half, crease and unfold (plain or white side face up)

2. Fold in both sides to meet in center, crease and unfold

3. Fold bottom right corner to center crease to form a triangle

4. Fold top right corner to meet first crease to form a smaller triangle

5. Fold top section into center, then fold over again

6. Fold bottom panel up to meet top panel to create case

7. Flip over and fold up bottom edge about 3/8" to close the bottom. Use glue stick or tape to seal it if you want it more durable

1.
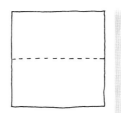

2.
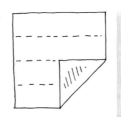

3.
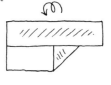

4.
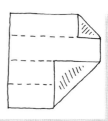

5.
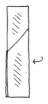

6.

7.
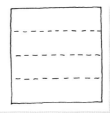

CHOPSTICK CASES 筷子盒
CONTINUED
STYLE 2

STEPS:

1. Hold paper horizontally and make center fold; open

2. Fold bottom left and right corners into center; open

3. Fold bottom left and right corners up to diagonal crease

4. Fold top left and right corners down to meet bottom flaps and crease

5. Fold left side and right side in to align with fold on top edge and form a triangle

6. Unfold top flaps and close again; you should have kite shape now

7. Fold the two top flaps down into the pouch so they hold down the inside flap

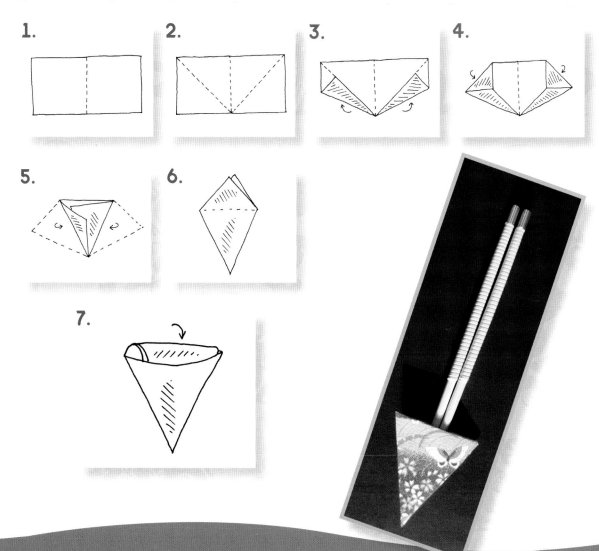

节日和假日

STYLE 3

STEPS:

1. Copy template for case on p. 113 on to cover weight paper. If you choose not to do the dragon design and draw your own, only use the contour lines

2. Color and decorate the design panel and the back panel

3. Cut out the case and fold on the inside seam

4. Tape the open bottom and right edges. Do it from the inside or use thin double stick tape if you don't want tape to show

5. If you want your case more festive, punch a hole in the top left corner and add a tassel, satin cord, charm or your own idea

HOW TO USE CHOPSTICKS:

1.

2.

3.

Rest one chopstick between your thumb and pointer fingers and hold steady with your middle and ring fingers

Add the second chopstick and hold like a pencil, gripping firmly with your thumb, pointer and middle fingers

Keep the bottom chopstick still with your thumb and open and close the tip of your top chopstick with your pointer and middle fingers. Time to eat!

CHOPSTiCK MANNERS

+ Do rest your chopsticks on the edge of a bowl or on a chopstick stand with the tips up when not eating and keep them parallel, not crossed

+ Don't stick chopsticks straight upright in a bowl of rice (this is a ritual only to honor the dead)

+ Don't tap or beat on your bowl with the chopsticks while eating (considered beggar behavior)

ALSO TRY

 Traditional Papermaking p. 20

 Papercuts p. 22

FESTIVAL LANTERN
节日灯笼

Chinese lanterns are a beautiful and important symbol of Chinese culture for holidays, festivals and also in daily life for lighting homes, shops and streets. They are designed and made in numerous sizes, shapes and styles from very simple tubes and globes to animal, geometric and flower shapes. Many efforts are made through Chinese museums and authentic lantern artisans to keep traditional lantern making techniques alive for future generations.

The lantern tradition started during East Han Dynasty (25 A.D.- 220 A.D.) and reached its peak during Tang (618 A.D.- 907 A.D.) and Song (960 A.D.- 1279 A.D.) Dynasties. Throughout their rich history lanterns have ranged from more plain and functional to extremely artistic with painted or papercut images, scenes and stories on the surfaces. The frames are crafted in a variety of woods, bamboo, reed and wire depending on the style.

This lantern design is adapted from the common red circular lanterns hung and displayed during the Lunar New Year. It resembles the "full moon" and has the lucky roundness of "yuan", Chinese money. It also can be carried with a stick by children during festival parades.

YOU'LL NEED:

MATERIALS:

• White poster board 22x28" sheet

• Black construction paper sheet 11x17" (or 2 smaller taped together)

• Gold or yellow paper sheet 11x17" (or 2 smaller taped together)

• Colored tissue paper including red

• Thin twine

• Stick or dowel for handle (optional)

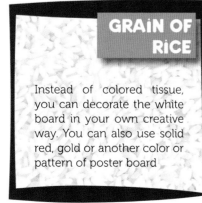

GRAIN OF RICE

Instead of colored tissue, you can decorate the white board in your own creative way. You can also use solid red, gold or another color or pattern of poster board

STEPS:

1. Cut 3 pieces poster board;

    16" x 12"
    28" x ¾"
    13" x 1"

Then cut black paper into 1" x 13" and 1 ½" x 16" strips, and yellow paper into a 13 ½" x 3 ½" piece

节日和假日

STEPS:

2. Take ripped scraps of tissue and glue them on to largest piece of board and 28" piece including a brushed light top coat of glue to secure and glaze it; let dry

3. Draw lines on 16" x 12" piece across top 1 ½" and bottom 1", fold creases on both lines and flatten back out

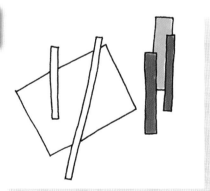

FESTIVAL LANTERN 节日灯笼
CONTINUED

4. Draw 1" lines for slats up to 1 ½" line and cut (only up to line!)

5. Take large piece with slats and connect top border in a ring overlapped and stapled for the top ring of the lantern

6. Connect longest piece together in a ring with staple or tape for the central lantern ring

7. Gently work inward curve into strips and staple middle ring about half way between folds, on the inside and starting at opposite four points on the ring. (Younger children may need help with this). There will be a gap between the strips that you should try and keep even all the way around

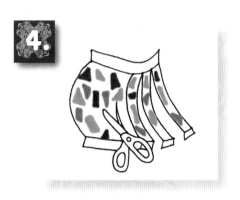

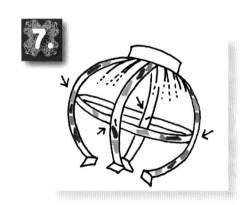

8. Staple together bottom 13" x 1" ring. Gather the bottom strips and staple on to the inside of the ring, overlapping them to fit

9. Cut thin fringe on long side of yellow paper leaving 1" at the top. Align black strip over 1" side of yellow paper and secure strip and fringe to bottom ring of lamp

10. Secure top black ring. Punch holes on opposite sides of top

11. Thread twine and tie to make hanging loop. Secure to stick with small attached string if desired

ALSO TRY

Mini-Lantern Garland p. 98

Lucky Lantern p. 56

节日和假日

LUCKY LANTERN 鸿运灯笼

While lanterns crafted in all styles and materials have been part of Chinese culture throughout history, many people of rural China today still rely on lanterns and lamps in the evenings to light their homes or to carry outside to check on their animals. These range from tin or bronze candle lanterns to wick lamps using oil, butter or kerosene for fuel. Lanterns, lamps and candlelight have also always been a symbolic part of spiritual and religious ceremonies.

This lantern, designed by my daughter, is a fast and simple project that will add a festive glow to your house during Chinese celebrations, or at any time. Perhaps you can imagine the glow of this lamp inside a small village home on an evening in China, with a passerby outside seeing the warm flickering light in the window.

YOU'LL NEED:

MATERIALS:

• Red paper 8 ½ x 11" sheet

• Wax paper 8 ½ x 11" sheet

• Aluminum foil 8 ½ x 11" sheet

• LED flicker votive or tea light (note- do NOT use real candle or anything that could be hot or flammable!)

STEPS:

1. Match up and glue together the red paper and tin foil sheets; smooth any foil wrinkles (foil helps reflect the light and keep lamp safe)

2. Gently fold in quarters with the foil on the inside, but don't make sharp creases. Cut shapes from the two folded edges only. You can sketch the cuts first if you want to position them well

3. Fold again and cut shapes on new folded side. Then carefully unfold and smooth wrinkles and creases on both sides

4. Tape together the short side with red paper on outside to form a cylinder

5. Wrap wax paper sheet around the outside and tape on same seam

6. Place over LED tea light and enjoy your lantern!

GRAIN OF RICE

You can make several lanterns and vary the paper color and style of cuts for an impressive display on a table, mantel or walkway

NOTE: These are decorative lanterns only! Do not use anything flammable inside or near the lantern or leave unattended when lit

Festivals & Holidays

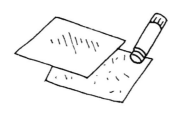 **1.**

Did You Know?

✦ Before lanterns were designed with flames and fuels, the ancient Chinese were known to capture fireflies in transparent containers to use for lamplight

节日和假日

2.

 3.

 4.

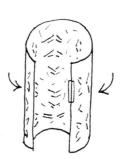

 **5.**

 6.

ALSO TRY

Festival Lantern p. 52

Mini-Lantern Garland p. 98

Papercut Designs p. 22

FLOATING DRAGON BOAT
划龙舟

During the Dragon Boat Festival on the 5th day of the 5th lunar month, Chinese people flock to the water to watch and participate in exciting and colorful dragon boat races. There are different styles of boat, but you can always expect the elongated shape, dramatic open-mouthed dragon head and scaled tail, with space inside for many paddlers. They were originally made of teak wood and are still considered some of the largest and most impressive flat water racing canoes in the world.

The paddling team is usually from ten to fifty people depending on the size of the boat with a drummer facing them. The drummer beats the rhythm for their strokes. A "sweep" paddler in the rear controls the boat's direction. The boat teams race to be first to grab the flag at the end of the course.

Now you can have your own dragon boat races if you make several boats with your friends. Tie some fishing line to them if you are in a place where they could float away. Remember to have adult supervision for children around any water- even in the tub!

YOU'LL NEED:

  • Colored pencils are better with moisture than markers

MATERIALS:
• Quart sized clean milk or juice carton
• White cover weight 8 ½" x 11" paper
• Clear waterproof packing tape
• Colored heavy waterproof (duct) tape
• Craft foam sheet
• 10 plastic drinking straws

STEPS:

1. Copy head and tail templates on p. 114 on to white cover weight paper and color in so both sides match

2. Cut drink carton in half the long way with the "v" at one end. Children should get an adult to help

3. Cut out the pieces and glue pairs together, leaving head flaps and tail base open to attach to carton. Flaps folded back will hold head to the flat end, and the tail will slip on at the "v" end

4. Glue head and tail on to carton with glue stick and cover them on both sides with clear packing tape. Then clean up by trimming around the edges leaving ¼" of clear edge to keep paper sealed

GRAIN OF RICE

You can add paddlers and a drum to have your race be more realistic. Just remember to use materials that are lightweight and can get a little wet!

5. Cover the carton sides with colored duct tape. You can then add designs in another color. (The tape rips easily along the grain if you want thin strips)

6. Punch 5 holes along each side, 1¼" apart from each other and ¼" from top edge

7. Use oar paddle template on p. 114 to trace ten paddles on craft foam. Cut them out and punch holes

8. Snip straws just below bend, thread on the paddles, and insert into boat sides

Did You Know?

✦ Before the race starts there is a ceremony where a local leader will dot the dragon boat head's eyes with red paint to "bring it to life"

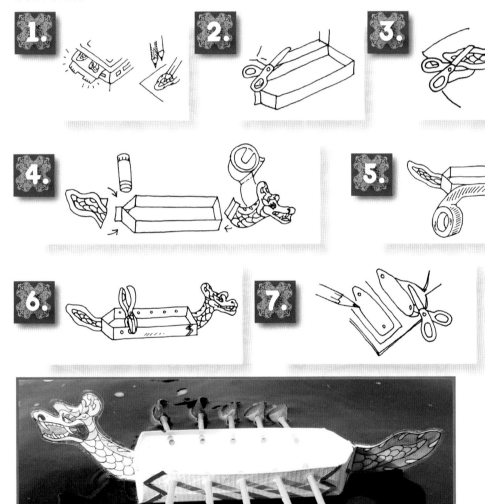

SCENTED INCENSE BAG
香囊

The Scented Sachet or Incense Bag (Xiang nang) is a small pouch worn on the body during holidays and events but especially the Dragon Boat (Duanwu) Festival. During the festival the sachet is tied at the waist or worn around the neck as a talisman to ward off evil spirits and bring good fortune. The pouch is also sewn onto young childrens' clothing.

Another use is for a young woman to show a man her interest as a gentle hint or promise, or as a love token between young couples. Today the Chinese still like to make sachets and women pass the folk skill down through the generations.

Traditionally it is made of woven five-color silk threads, tiny fragments of fabric or wrapped in silk cloth. Often a design is also embroidered onto it. The pouch is filled with different kinds of Chinese spices or aromatic herbs such as cinnabar, realgar, wormwood and mugwort. You can make this simple pouch or design your own shape. Symbolic animals, figures, heart, water drop and butterfly are common shapes and care is always given to the color and design.

YOU'LL NEED:

• Common pins

MATERIALS:
• 1 ft. silk or decorative fabric
• Matching thread and needle (sharp, use caution!)
• Colored thread (like embroidery thread) for tassel
• 1 ft. satin cord for drawstring
• Aromatic herbs or spice that you like to put in pouch (potpourri, cloves, cinnamon stick pieces, dried garden herbs)

STEPS:

1. Trace pattern on p. 115 on thin or tracing paper and cut out

2. Pin to fabric and cut out shape

3. Cut slits along top where marked (If stitching design, do so before sewing sides)

4. Fold with insides out and sew a simple straight stitch along the sides leaving top open

GRAIN OF RICE

You can add your own touch to the pouch front with embroidery, glued on embellishments or fabric markers

5. Fold right side out and weave cord through slits to create drawstring; knot the end

6. Tie a small bunch of colored thread in the middle and fold. Wrap tie together near the top to create a broom-style tassel; sew on to bottom of pouch

7. Fill with your chosen scent

节日和假日

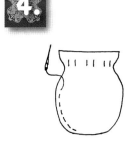

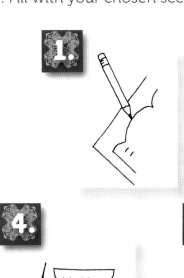

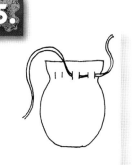

Double fish design (to stitch) is on template p. 115

PERFORMANCE & DANCE

RIBBON DANCE STICK

绸带舞的绸带

The Chinese ribbon dance started being performed during the Han Dynasty (206 B.C.E. - 420 C.E.) and began with dancers simply holding thin strips of silk ribbon in their hands. Later during the Tang Dynasty (618 A.D.- 906 A.D.) the dance style became very popular and the ribbon strips grew in length and became attached to sticks for better control.

This dance was originally performed only for royalty, to music. Large and flowing movements of the ribbon were accompanied by slow music while sharp movements when the ribbon was flicked and snapped were accompanied by faster music depending on the choreography.

One or both hands holding ribbon sticks can be used in the dance, and the length of the ribbon can vary. Today ribbon dances are performed in cultural festivals all over the world and are known as Cai Dai Wu Dao.

YOU'LL NEED:

MATERIALS:

• Red material (wide ribbon, cut satin, felt or other fabric that moves well) 2-3 "x 54-60". Ribbons can be any pattern or color but red is traditional

• 10-14" wooden dowel for handle; pre-cut wooden dowels can be found at your local craft store and 3/8" diameter works well. (Note: have adult cut to size if using sharp tool)

• Paint or decorating materials if desired

• Red or black duct style strong tape (If you don't want to use duct tape to hold the ribbon in place you can use a wood glue and cover the end with ribbon or cord for decoration)

STEPS:

1. If you cut a dowel to size, sand the ends to avoid splinters. You may leave the dowel plain, paint/color it or use a shine coating material

2. Wrap ribbon or fabric around stick end, approximately 2" down; you can use a few dots of glue to start fabric on stick to make it more secure when dry

GRAIN OF RICE

The ribbon dance is usually meant for multiple dancers so gather your friends and start synchronizing your moves! Wearing the same costume makes your dance even more impressive

Performance & Dance

表演和舞蹈

STEPS:

3. Tape end of fabric to stick with multiple wraps so it is secure

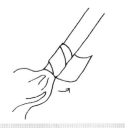

ALSO TRY

Dragon Parade Costume p. 36

Lion Dance Mask p. 70

RIBBON DANCE STICK
绸带舞的绸带

These ribbon stick movements can be done with your dance steps:

 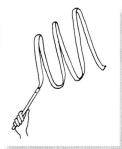 

Many ancient sculptures from the Han and Tang dynasties of the earliest long sleeve dancers have been recovered

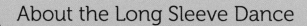

About the Long Sleeve Dance

It is widely believed that the Long Sleeve Dance came from a man who saved a Han Dynasty emperor from an assassination attempt by blocking the attacker's sword with the silk from his sleeve. A "long sleeve dance" was done in gratitude, and over time became inspiration for the ribbon dance.

In ancient China, the Long Sleeve Dance was performed for royalty and officials to celebrate the grandest occasions. Women wearing dresses with long, elegant sleeves would dance expressively to imitate the movement of fairies, and the gentle ripples of water. The dancers used their silk sleeves to accentuate hand and arm movements, whirling them around gracefully and snapping them like whips.

The Long Sleeve Dance combines Chinese Peking Opera and classic Chinese dance. The sleeves of the costumes are made of special silk and can be 80 inches long. The extremely long sleeves also date back to ancient moral conduct, which promoted covering the entire body from sunlight.

Performance & Dance

Did You Know?

+ The ribbon and sleeve dances are performed to express many emotions. The ribbons and sleeves are "extended arms" which under careful control, can embody freedom, happiness, sadness and love

HOW TO DANCE:

• Listening to the rhythm and mood of the music is the most important part of this traditional dance. All twirls, tosses and body movement should be synchronized with the rhythm of the song and in most traditional Chinese music this will be easy to follow

• The pace will also affect the artistry of your routine. Large, flowing movements are ideal for slow music as your ribbon "floats" above your body. When the music speeds up, sharp, quick movements of the arm(s) will give the look of "fluttering wings" that will bring a different kind of beauty to your dance

• While you allow the music to inspire your movements, try not to let the ribbons get tangled or touch the floor

• There are many specific Chinese steps and dances that you can learn but follow these suggestions to practice and repeat your movements and get you started

OTHER TYPES OF DANCER'S RIBBONS

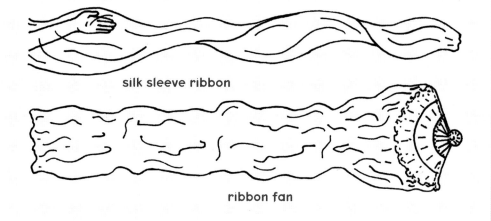

silk sleeve ribbon

ribbon fan

DRAGON PUPPET 龙形木偶

You will see the dragon theme, symbol and image again and again in Chinese culture. This mythical animal is not only believed to bring good fortune and ward off evil spirits but most Chinese people believe they are descendants of the dragon.

This is a simplified, modern version of the Chinese rod puppet, a folk art puppet style that emerged nearly 2000 years ago with great attention given to both the artistry and performance. Traditionally the head was wooden with one main rod handle and often other rods for the hands. It can be used with a simple shelf stage and combined with other styles of puppets for a performance.

YOU'LL NEED:

MATERIALS:
- Red bond or construction paper 8 ½ x 11"
- White cover weight paper 8 ½ x 11"
- 2 large sized craft sticks or bamboo skewers
- Optional- glitter, sequins on head and tail
- You can also add dangling ribbons or curled paper to the body

STEPS:

1. Copy templates on pp. 116 & 117 on as heavy a paper as possible

2. Cut out head and tail sides and decorate

3. Cut the red paper in half in the long direction and tape the strips lengths together so you have a 4 ¼" x 22" piece. Accordion fold the paper

4. Arrange the head and tail on the accordion paper ends. Position the stick handles on the back sides. Glue the two head sides and two tail sides on to the body ends with the sticks inside

GRAIN OF RICE

See the different ways you can control and move the puppet's accordion body to make your dragon come alive

Performance & Dance

表演和舞蹈

 1.

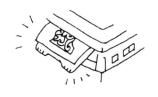

 2.

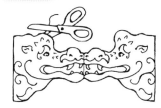

Did You Know?

+ Famous Chinese inventor and mechanical engineer Ma Jun was the first to make early wooden puppets have movement at the request of Emperor Ming of Wei. He connected the puppet parts to a hidden handmade wooden waterwheel with a current

 3.

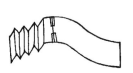

4.

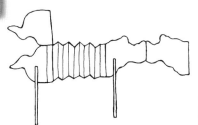

ALSO TRY

 Shadow Puppets
p. 76

 Dragon Parade Costume p. 36

LION DANCE MASK 舞狮的面具

The lion dance dates back to the Han Dynasty (205 B.C. to 220 A.D) and is still an important Chinese tradition. Usually the dance is part of festivities like the Chinese Lunar New Year, grand openings of businesses, weddings and other significant occasions. If performed well, the lion dance is believed to bring luck, happiness, harmony and prosperity.

Dance troupes and martial artists are often hired to perform and drummers and cymbal players accompany the lion movements with a tremendous racket, meant to scare away all evil spirits. For payment, the lion often is offered a head of lettuce with "lucky money" tied to it and ceremoniously "eats" the greens.

This mask project design is intended for young people to dance as a group with individual masks rather than with only two people forming the lion head and body. This is a non-traditional twist but works well for young dancers performing and learning about Chinese culture and many of the traditional "lion" moves can be adapted.

The mask artwork can be either very creative or more traditional. It is held by the handles and moved around your face and body in front of you so it should be large and sturdy, with colorful and expressive facial features.

YOU'LL NEED:

- Glue gun (use only with adult supervision) or strong glue
- Hammer   • Bucket/paste tub

MATERIALS:

- Lots of newspaper (some torn into strips, some crumpled)
- Flour (or paper mache paste- see Grain of Rice)
- Water
- Plastic shopping bag
- Aluminum foil
- Grommets (4) with 3/8" minimum hole (sold at fabric stores)
- Rope/cord for handles that fits holes (approx. 14" length for each handle)
- Decorations- fringe, feather boas, pom-poms, sequins, etc..
- Craft paint- bright colors and black
- Thick cardboard (from packing carton is fine)
- Shine coating (optional)

GRAIN OF RICE

The flour paste works well, but craft store boxed paper mache powder mixed with water produces a little nicer result

Performance & Dance

Shape of mask head contour and mouthpiece

STEPS:

1. Mix flour with water at 1 to 2 ratio and stir until lumps are mostly dissolved; put aside to thicken

2. Stuff and squish a plastic bag with crumpled newspaper inside to build an oval "face" shape and ideally, adhere it to a flat, hard work surface with tape. You are building your "armature" or form that will shape the mask, and should cover most of your face

3. Add newspaper wads, cardboard or egg carton cups to "build" features and tape securely. Cover the whole surface with foil, making sure all your shapes and detail are pressed and showing

 1.

 2.

 3.

ALSO TRY

Dragon Parade Costume p. 36

Ribbon Dance Stick p. 64

✱ Note the photo in the tab- it's a lion dance head!

STEPS:

4. Apply paper mache strips one by one that are moistened in your flour glue (run strips through fingers to remove excess), overlapping and covering all areas including edges near work surface. Layer on gradually (3 or 4 layers), smoothing as you go and keeping strips from sticking up or getting lumpy in the wrong areas. Allow to dry

5. Remove stuffing carefully so as not to rip the mask. Trim around edge to clean it up (this mask does not need eye holes)

6. Hammer grommets in four spots for handle holes, or punch holes and reinforce a different way. This step may require help from an adult.

7. Cut "mouth" shape from cardboard and glue in a "flap" position to the inside of the mask

8. Draw on face design (sketch out first on paper if easier) and paint. You can also paint a solid color on the inside so the whole mask is covered. You can look online for traditional face designs

9. After mask is dry, glue on decorations and thread and knot handles with cord

Performance & Dance

表演和舞蹈

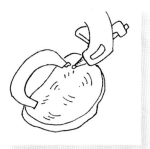 **7.**

 8.

9.

There are two styles of traditional lion dance from northern and southern China. The northern style lion has a shaggy mane and four legs and is more realistic. It uses prancing legs and is more acrobatic and entertaining

The southern lion has a drape body and can have two or four legs. The head appears more like a dragon's than a lion's but without long dragon horns or a long snout. It makes dramatic head thrusts and dips to the sound of drums and gongs as it dances in a more symbolic, ceremonial style

CIRCLE FAN 工艺扇

China has been called the "kingdom of fans" as they are a rich part of the culture and there is a long history of hand crafting, producing and exporting fans worldwide. Fans have taken every shape and design and have been made of materials such as bamboo, feathers, paper, palms, silk, sandalwood and precious stone.

Since the Yin Dynasty 3000 years ago when they were used to keep sun and sand off the emperors, the finest fans have been crafted with elaborate artistry combining weaving, knotting, calligraphy, embroidery and painted lacquer. Fans are also made and used for traditional dance and are adorned to fit the performance and costumes.

This project combines two Chinese fan styles; the round fan and the pleated fan. You can decide how to decorate your fan as you'll see from the suggestions. Can you come up with a traditional Chinese theme for your artwork?

YOU'LL NEED:

 • Art materials for your design on the fan paper (paint, colored pencils, etc...)

MATERIALS:

• Paper- approx. 5 1/2" x 34" note- two 11 x 17" sheets taped together and cut will make two long fan strips *(use white construction, watercolor or heavy rice paper if you plan to paint your own design)*
• 2 large craft sticks, plain or colored

Here is a watercolor brush paint design with some gold pen on the edge

STEPS:

1. Cut your paper to size and tape together if needed, to make a 34" x 5 1/2" strip

2. Draw, paint, stamp, write calligraphy, or any other technique to decorate your fan

3. Glue on the two stick handles on the back, on the top half of each end of the paper

4. On the back, mark out the edge lightly with pencil at each 1" and fold accordion style. You can use a ruler to help crease the folds

5. Gather the bottom pleats of the fan and tape together

6. Gently work a curve into the pleats so the fan curls around to a circle and the handles meet

GRAIN OF RICE

You can fancy up the handles if you are carrying or dancing with your fan by wrapping them together with colored cord or shiny ribbon in a coil that is tied or taped securely and even adding a tassel

Performance & Dance

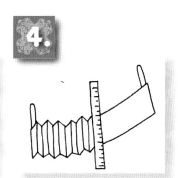

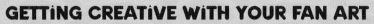

GETTING CREATIVE WITH YOUR FAN ART

You can do anything to make your fan special. Just remember that it will have pleated folds, so detailed designs or small calligraphy may be hard to enjoy

- Zodiac animal theme- see designs on p. 126 and make a pattern from one or many
- Paint with splatter, pattern or wet washes
- Draw a scene like a scroll
- Do a Chinese brush painting style like the example here
- Use rubber stamps, chop art or homemade stamping

ALSO TRY

Brush Painted Scroll p. 14

Ribbon Dance Stick p. 64

Chop Art p. 18

表演和舞蹈

75

SHADOW PUPPETS 皮影戏

Chinese shadow puppetry is an ancient form of storytelling and performance. It was originated in Xi'an during the Han Dynasty (206 B.C.- 220 A.D.) when it's believed that Emperor Wu was so saddened by the death of his love, a simple play with shadows was performed by a court member to bring his spirits back so he could rule his kingdom.

Shadow puppets are jointed for movement and were originally made of paper-thin donkey or cowhide cut into detailed silhouettes. They are famous in many parts of the world but China has its own special style and history. They were designed for traveling from village to village with a simple and compact stage, collapsed puppets and a small performing troupe providing music and storytelling. Oil lamps were used to illuminate the stage area so even the most remote locations could come alive with music and performance.

The figures of people and animals are usually designed in profile (called the half face) to show the most expression and movement across the stage. Sometimes there is translucent color that appears when illuminated on the thinnest parts or cutouts on the puppet, along with the solid dark shadows. Today people still perform with traditional shadow puppets in an effort for this folk culture to be carried on.

YOU'LL NEED:

MATERIALS:

- Lightweight board (black poster board works well for shadows)
- Brass fasteners
- Bamboo skewers (2)
- Bendable plastic straws (4)
- Colored tissue paper (optional)

GRAIN OF RICE

For the puppet joints if you don't have brass fasteners, you can attach them with small chenille stem pieces pinched in half

1.

2.

Performance & Dance

STEPS:

1. Copy the two templates on pp. 118-119

2. Place template pieces on board or transfer directly on to it and cut contours and details (get adult help if using sharp cutting instruments). If you want colored panels, cut out the interior areas too (you can start them by punching a hole)

3. Punch holes in the marked spots at the joints

4. Place the fasteners through matching holes at joints and bend open to hold the pieces together

5. Attach main bamboo stick to lower middle of puppets and short end of bendable straws to arms (Mulan) and legs (horse). If you have interior panels, adhere colored tissue paper from the back

SHADOW PUPPETS 皮影戏
CONTINUED

THE STORY OF MULAN:

Mulan was a young woman in China with bravery and beauty. When her elderly father, a retired general was called by the emperor to protect against the invading Huns, she disguised herself as a boy (Fa Ping) to take her father's place. She asked for protection from the ancestors and a magical baby dragon appeared to guide her.

Mulan fought valiantly in the war with her coat of armor hiding her female identity for several years. When the war ended, she was offered an award of riches to work for the emperor, but all she wished for was a good horse and to return home.

Her family was was still alive and well when she arrived. Mulan gave her uniform to her little brother and returned to being a beautiful young woman, knowing that with love and courage, nothing was impossible.

PUTTiNG ON YOUR SHOW:

Any legend or story can be acted out but here is the basic traditional storyline of Mulan (Wu Mulan in China). You can make additional puppet designs including Mulan in armor disguised as a boy, her father, and the protective dragon to act out the whole story.

These puppets are in silhouette, however if you make them on light colored board, you can draw and decorate the characters and introduce the cast before they go behind the stage into shadow. You can also make props, buildings and landscape as silhouettes like the puppets with small stands on the back. Even a simple mountain will add an interesting setting as the characters travel across the stage.

GRAiN OF RiCE

If you want to rehearse your show, put a mirror in the audience area so you can see the shadow side!

Performance & Dance

MAKING the STAGE:

Many styles of puppet stages will work, as long as you have a surface of white paper or fabric covering the opening for the puppet shadows. This very simple tabletop stage only requires folded corrugated cardboard and a large sheet of white paper or lightweight white fabric mounted to it.

Dimensions: 48" x 36" Fold side flaps at 12"

1. Cut out frame hole in the middle panel leaving 1 ½" on each side, 2" on the top and 3 ½" on the bottom (have an adult help with the cutting)

2. Adhere white thin paper or fabric slightly larger than the frame hole on the back side of the stage

3. Decorate the front of the stage if desired

4. Set up a light source behind the stage and puppets

Did You Know?

+ A typical Chinese shadow puppet troupe has four to seven members operating the puppets, adding vocal sounds and playing instruments, but only one, named the "singer" is the lead speaker of all the parts

表演和舞蹈

Note:
Use caution if handling an electric light and do not leave it unattended around paper or fabric materials

ALSO TRY

Dragon Puppet
p. 68

MONKEY KING MASK

美猴王面具

The Monkey King (Sun Wukong) is a favorite character of children in China and comes from a novel titled <u>Journey to the West</u> written by Wu Cheng'en during the Ming Dynasty (c. 1500- 1582). The story is based on a real monk, Xuanzang and his long journey to India to bring back the sacred Buddhist sutra to China. The Monkey King was created as the character that guides his journey.

The story was also made into a famous opera that is still performed today. Many are delighted by the Monkey King because his many different traits make him interesting and entertaining. He is kind and friendly but can also cause harm with his mischief and combative nature. He is first a monkey but then turns immortal and embodies all kinds of magical powers. He is originally focused on his selfish desires but in the end helps the Buddhist monk.

Although we have one fable here, there are many widely known Chinese legends about the Monkey King involving folklore, religion, philosophy and satire. This mask combines the monkey animal traits with the theatrical decoration of classic Chinese opera. Young children will enjoy making it as a simple mask, while older kids and teens may want to write a script for a full production with all the characters.

YOU'LL NEED:

MATERIALS:

• Cover weight white paper

• Elastic thread, yarn or twine

STEPS:

1. Copy template on p. 120 on to white cover weight paper

2. Color in mask with bright colors

3. Cut out around contour of mask and cut out eye holes carefully

4. Punch or poke holes through the sides where marked. Tie on elastic thread or two pieces of yarn or string to wear mask

GRAIN OF RICE

You can make another style of mask by leaving off the elastic and holes and gluing a craft stick on to one side for a handle to hold it to your face

Performance & Dance

表演和舞蹈

THE STORY OF THE MONKEY KiNG:

The fable begins with the Monkey King being born from the earth as a stone monkey. He joined the other monkeys that dared anyone to enter a cave behind the waterfall leading to the heavens. The stone monkey was the only one to go so they declared him Monkey King. Through this journey he learned the secrets of martial arts, found magical powers and achieved immortality. He also got his clothing and long gold "magical staff" from the reluctant Dragons of the Ocean.

The Monkey King went back and taught his monkey friends these arts, but also behaved in a greedy way, needing to always have the most and attract attention. He also indulged on food and drink. As he journeyed through many lands on earth and in the immortal heavens, he started many conflicts and angered many gods who were all too weak to control him.

Finally the gods ask Buddha to help them because the Monkey King was immortal and could not be killed. Buddha trapped him for five hundred years under a huge mountain. At the end of this time Xuanzang, a Buddhist monk was about to make his pilgrimage across China to India to find and bring back the sutra.

The Jade Emperor of Heaven with the help of a goddess summoned the Monkey King from his place beneath the mountain to be a guide for the monk. They were joined by two companions willing to give up their evil ways to take the journey, Pigsy, a fierce and lazy pig and Sandy, a water monster that transformed into a quiet muscular figure.

Together they made their journey to India with the monk. Along the way, the Monkey King was filled with antics of mischief, deceit and disobedience but also used his immortal powers to help the monk fight demons and monsters to reach his destination and bring back the sutra. In the end the Monkey King showed that he had a good and generous heart.

ALSO TRY

Dragon Parade
Costume p. 36

Lion Dance Mask
p. 70

Chinese Folk Toys & Games

中国民间玩具

CHiNESE FOLK
TOYS & GAMES

RATTLE HAND DRUM

拨浪鼓

Many styles of rattle drums and noise makers are used by both adults and children in China. They have a long history as percussion instruments and toys as well as for making noise at gatherings and events. The two heads of the early drums were usually made from animal skin or oiled paper with a wooden body.

This simple version of the traditional musical folk toy makes wonderful rhythm when the handle is spun back and forth. The drum faces can be decorated with Chinese characters, zodiac animal symbols or any type of artwork you want to create. Then go ahead and make some noise!

YOU'LL NEED:

MATERIALS:

- Small white paper plates
- Yarn
- Large craft stick
- Pony beads

STEPS:

1. Punch two holes in each plate opposite each other

2. Decorate both plate panels on bottom side; with artwork or other decorations

3. Knot two yarn strands at one end and thread on beads

4. Match plates, bottom sides out and thread yarn through holes. Tie securely being sure the length is right for the bead to hit the drum face

5. Slip handle in between plates and secure with tape

GRAIN OF RICE

You can put dry beans or rice between the plates before sealing for added shake and rattle noise!

中国民间玩具

Did You Know?

+ A rattle drum has also been called a "peddler drum" because its musical noise could attract attention with a peddler's rhythmic call to hawk his wares

3.

4.

5.

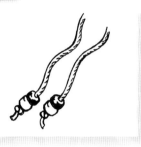

ALSO TRY

 Yo-yo p. 102

DIAMOND KITE 风筝

China is the birthplace of the first kite designs that ever took flight over 2000 years ago. Generals used them to measure distance, spy, or fly with noisemakers to scare off the enemy. Later during the Tang Dynasty (618 A.D.- 906 A.D.) kites became popular recreation for royals and aristocrats.

Other legends about the earliest kite flying include wanting to imitate the sails of fishing boats or the fluttering wings of flying birds and insects. Originally made of silk and bamboo, the invention of paper made kites a more common handicraft. The symbolic designs displayed artwork from Chinese folklore or history.

Some Chinese believe that the higher the kite is flown the more prosperous they will become. Many also seek the restorative powers of looking up at a kite to improve eyesight while opening the mouth to rid the body of excess heat for a Yin-Yang balance with the fresh air.

Many kite styles such as centipede and winged designs are still finely crafted and used in China, especially in Weifang, Shandong Province, a city rich in kite history. Here we have a familiar kite design that is fun and quite simple for you to make and fly.

YOU'LL NEED:

- Paint or markers to decorate sail (optional)
- Glue (optional)
- Small knife for grooves (with adult help)

MATERIALS:

- Lightweight paper, fabric or thin plastic larger than dowel frame (13 gallon tall kitchen bag cut open works well and is white for decorating)

- Two wooden dowels 3/16" or ¼" diameter, 30" and 36" in length

- Tail material- wide ribbon, cloth strips, paper strips or streamers

- Thin twine for frame construction

- Thin twine on reel or winder to fly kite

GRAIN OF RICE

Apply a dot of glue from a bottle or glue gun at each point where the twine connects with the frame or knots for extra strength

PARTS OF A KiTE

SPINE- vertical main stick of frame

SPAR- horizontal cross stick (flat or bowed) of frame

BRIDLE- string attached to spine and spar to anchor surface of kite and control in air

TAIL- long strips of paper, ribbon or tie cloth attached to base point to stabilize flight

SAIL- paper, plastic or cloth surface that is attached to the frame

WINDER OR REEL- hand held piece used to wind your flying line

TOWLINE- flying line connected to the kite and the reel

STEPS:

1. Carve small grooves around ends of dowels ¼" down to help hold the twine frame in place. Any serrated blade works fine on the soft wood

2. Tie twine to one groove on spar (30" piece) and bend gently to make a bowed curve. Then tie other end to hold it securely and trim excess

3. Cross dowels leaving 14" at the top of the long spine dowel and tie the joint securely, making sure your dowels are at a right angle

4. Tie end of long twine around bottom groove of spine dowel. Then wind the twine around all four sides, tying it firmly at each groove and back to the base to create a diamond frame for the sail

5. Cut sail material using the frame as a pattern, leaving an extra inch on all sides. Lay flat and decorate sail surface if desired

6. Wrap sail edges one by one around string frame and tape down as smoothly as possible. Doing opposite edges at a time will help make a tighter surface

7. Make bridle by tying 40" of twine first to the top of the spine dowel, bringing it to the front. Then put a square of tape on the sail to reinforce the lower spot, halfway between the cross joint and bottom. Cut a slit in the tape to thread the twine through to the back. Tie off on the spine dowel

8. You now have a large arc of string at the front of the kite. Make a loop slightly up from the middle and attach reel

9. Attach tail at the kite base. It can be longer or shorter depending on how the kite reacts to the weight. You are ready to fly!

  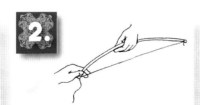

  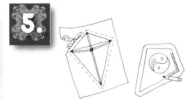 

✱ See Project Resources section for more information on kite history

ABACUS 算盘

This notable Chinese invention is a well-known counting tool from about 1200 A.D. during the Yuan Dynasty. Also called "suan pan" (calculating plate) this construction of simple beads and rods in a frame has been used widely since ancient times for all sorts of mathematical equations. The traditional design includes two decks within the frame and thirteen rods. The top deck (heaven) has two beads and bottom deck (earth) has five.

Even in China today, school children learn abacus skills and you can still find shopkeepers and vendors that calculate this way with their customers. Once your abacus is made, see how skilled and fast you can get with solving problems as the ancient Chinese did and how high you can go with your calculations.

YOU'LL NEED:

MATERIALS:

- 13 bamboo skewers cut to 5" long
- 91 pony beads
- Corrugated cardboard
- Craft paint

STEPS:

1. Measure and cut out 5 cardboard pieces: (2) at 10" x 3½", (2) at 1 ¼" x 5¼", and (1) at 10" x 7/8" (note cardboard grain direction on two largest for easiest folding)

2. Draw vertical guide lines on largest two pieces (for top and base) for ½", 1¼", ½", and 1¼" sections across width. Score and start bend of folds

3. Paint all pieces making sure to cover all sides and edges. Save your extra paint! You will need it for touch-ups later

4. Measure and poke 13 holes ½" from each end and ¾" apart from each other on one of the

HOW TO CALCULATE WiTH AN ABACUS

The column values from RIGHT to LEFT are: Ones, Tens, Hundreds, Thousands, Ten thousands, Hundred thousands, continuing up a digit for each rod

Upper deck beads have value of "5", lower deck beads of "1"

To count and calculate, lay abacus flat and move beads down from upper deck (with index finger) and up from lower deck (with thumb) toward beam

large end panels, along center of 10 x 1 ¼" section; repeat on other end panel. Now do the same on middle beam piece

5. Fold, join and tape together long seams on two large end pieces

6. Assemble by sticking skewers into holes, threading 5 beads on each, sliding beam piece on to 1" down from top, threading 2 beads on each and putting on other end

7. Tape the side panels on at the corners

8. Touch up the paint over tape areas and any missed spots

9. Lay flat, move beads away from ends and put a small dot of glue at each skewer hole. Then let dry

Did You Know?

+ The abacus has also been used as a valuable tool for blind people to learn math skills through touch rather than sight

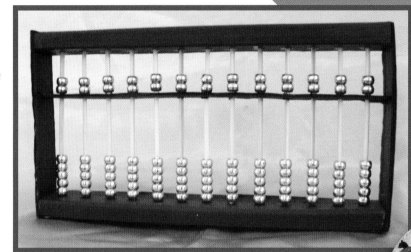

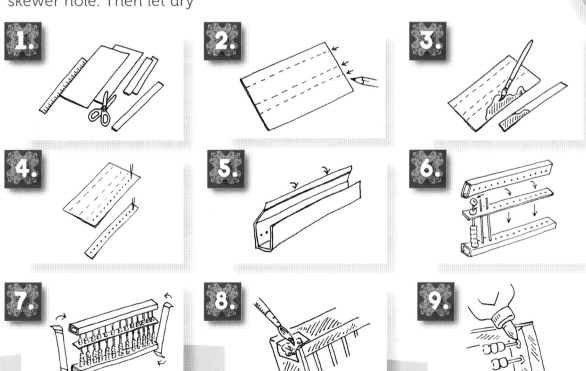

SHUTTLECOCK 毽子

Shuttlecock (jianzi) is a popular folk game in China which you will see played in parks and other public areas by both children and adults. To play, you keep the shuttlecock in the air using different parts of the body except the hands. This ancient sport originated in the Han Dynasty (206 B.C.- 220 A.D.) and grew in the T'ang Dynasty (618 A.D.- 906 A.D.). It was eventually so widespread that there were shops that only made and sold shuttlecocks.

Shuttlecocks were originally crafted with rooster feathers attached to a Chinese coin with cloth sewn around it, a tradition that still exists today. However they are also now manufactured for purchase in other materials. People still enjoy the sport for exercise, socializing and because it can be played so easily in any location.

In the Ming Dynasty (1368-1644) the first official shuttlecock kicking competitions were organized in China. The shuttlecock sport has spread around the world because of a Chinese athlete from Jiangsu that performed a demonstration at the Berlin Olympic Games in 1936, and later in 1984 it became an official Chinese national sport. See the game instructions on p. 130 to learn how to play authentic shuttlecock games with your friends.

YOU'LL NEED:

MATERIALS:

- Colored heavy tape like duct tape
- Plastic straw trimmed to 2"
- Cardboard (such as cereal box)
- 3-5 pennies (or metal washers)
- 3-5 large colored feathers

STEPS:

1. Draw and cut out two circles from cardboard about 2" in diameter (trace something with a round end or cap for nice circles)

2. Punch a hole in center of one cardboard circle

3. Cut four slits on one end of straw 1" down

GRAIN OF RICE

You can decorate the base by covering entirely with colored tape, applying stickers or creating a design with different colored tapes

4. Stick the straw into the cardboard circle hole and spread and flatten the four sliced pieces; tape down securely

5. Place the two cardboard circles together with the coins and taped straw ends on the inside and tape sealed. The straw end should be sticking straight up on the outside

6. Put a few drops of white glue in straw and stick the feathers in firmly; let dry

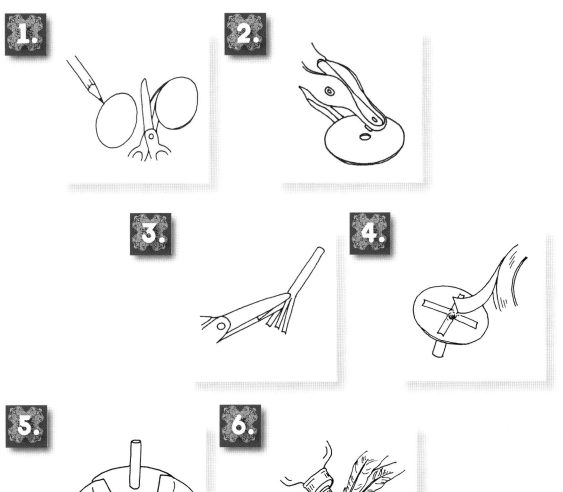

ALSO TRY

Yo-yo p. 102

Floating Dragon Boat p. 58

TANGRAM 七巧板

The tangram is an ancient Chinese "wisdom puzzle" with a mysterious history. There are diagrams and writings on tangrams discovered from as early as 1813 but little is known about the true origin which was probably much earlier. It is the most famous of all Chinese puzzles and has been enjoyed by everyday people, scholars and wealthy emperors alike.

Tangrams consist of seven specific geometric pieces called "tans". Although the pieces making up the square are quite simple, there are many different ways to arrange them to create pictures, puzzles and designs. Long ago, elaborate game sets with cases were crafted from jade, ivory and precious stone along with simpler sets from paper or wood.

You can either measure and draw your own tangram from a square or copy the template provided. There are hundreds of designs you can make but here are three to get you started.

YOU'LL NEED:

MATERIALS:

• Heavy paper, card stock or tag board 8 ½ x 11" any color

STEPS:

1. Either copy the template on p. 121 or draw out a 6" square

2. If you draw it yourself, follow the pattern shown below to draw the sections. Be sure to draw the angles and lines exactly like the diagram. Drawing out a light grid of 4 by 4 squares (1 ½" each) first will make it easier

3. Cut the pieces apart neatly on the lines

4. Now you are ready to try some designs!

GRAIN OF RICE

If you create a design you like, you can glue it down in position on to a background sheet and hang it up or start a collection!

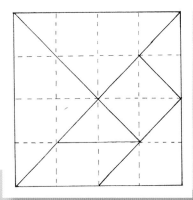

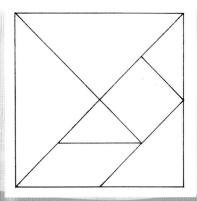

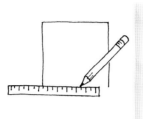

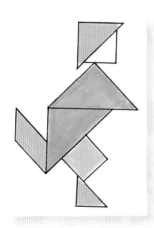

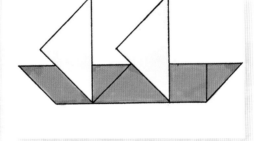

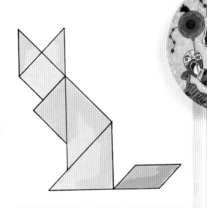

Rice Farmer　　　　　　Junk Boat　　　　　　Siamese Cat

HOW TO PLAY A TANGRAM PUZZLE GAME

Pick a finished shape and provide the outline or solid picture without the sections showing to all the players. See who can first fit the pieces into the shape after reading the classic rules to the players:

- All 7 pieces must be used
- All pieces must lie flat
- All pieces must touch
- No pieces may overlap
- Pieces may be rotated and/or flipped to form the shape

SIMPLE ASIAN CRAFTS

CLIMBING PANDA
爬树熊猫

The Giant Panda is considered a national treasure in China. Pandas are a member of the bear family and in Chinese are called xióng māo (熊猫) meaning "bear-cat", because they look like a bear in shape and a cat in face.

Today there are only about 1000 Giant Pandas living in the wild and they're mostly located in south-central China. The rest are protected and bred in wildlife refuges in China. The panda is listed on the International Union for Conservation of Nature's Red List of Threatened Animals, and is still endangered and decreasing in numbers.

Have your panda climb up and down your "tree", looking for bamboo, finding a napping place or just enjoying the view!

YOU'LL NEED:

MATERIALS:
• White cover weight stock 8 ½ x 11"
• Bamboo chopstick, 12" dowel or 12" wood ruler for "climbing tree"

STEPS:

1. See template on p. 122 and copy to cover weight paper

2. Color in illustrated side with colored pencils or markers

3. Cut contour of panda/bamboo art following template copy (Only cut around outside edge! Other lines are for detail and coloring)

4. Carefully cut slits on 6 dotted lines to the width needed for "tree" to slide through

5. Thread your wooden stick from the front as shown so paws are on top and have fun sliding your panda up and down!

✱ See the Project Resources section for how you can help the Great Pandas of China

Simple Asian Crafts

简单亚洲手工

Did You Know?

+ Up to 99 percent of a panda's diet is bamboo? However they only digest and get nutrition from about 20 percent of what they consume. As a result, pandas spend a lot of their time eating, and also sleeping, often in trees, to rest up for more eating!

 1.

 2.

3.

4.

5.

MINI-LANTERN GARLAND 小红灯笼

Decorating with a Chinese theme for festivals and celebrations can be easy and fun with this lantern garland. You've probably seen this popular lantern craft before and it's simple to reduce the lanterns in size to string and hang indoors or outdoors. You can adjust the size of the lanterns and length of the garland to fit your space.

YOU'LL NEED:

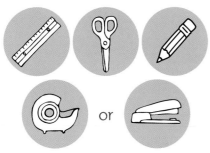

or

MATERIALS:

• Several sheets red paper
(text, cover or construction paper all work well) 5 ½" x 8 ½"

• Twine, yarn or thin ribbon at least 6 ft. long

STEPS:

1. Cut a sheet of paper into ¾" x 5 ½" strips for handles. Fold other sheets lengthwise and mark off 1" across the open edge for a "stop cutting" line

2. Measure ½" lines along the fold up to the 1" line; then cut from the fold side, being careful to stop at the line and not to cut through to the end

GRAIN OF RICE

If you are having friends over or hosting a birthday party this is a great craft to make and hang together. Using different patterned large origami papers can be especially attractive

3. Wrap around into a tube and tape or staple the top and bottom together (you can fold backwards first if you have cutting lines that you don't want to show)

Simple Asian Crafts

簡単亜洲手工

4. Secure the handle to the top in two spots with tape or staples; it looks nicer to attach on the inside of the lantern top

5. Tie lanterns to string by the handles making sure they are evenly spaced apart from each other

 1.

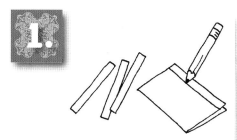

 2.

3.

4.

 5.

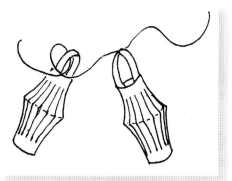

ALSO TRY

Lucky Lantern
p. 56

Festival Lantern
p. 52

Celebration
Garland p. 34

RATTAN FOLDED BRACELET 藤圈手镯

This simple bracelet requires very little in supplies and skill so can be used in any setting. The art of paper folding is traditionally Asian while the colors can echo the Chinese flag or Asian decorative arts. Thinner strips (1/2" to 1") can be used and will create a slimmer, more detailed bracelet. Also shiny gold or patterned paper can add sparkle and interest to your bracelet- just watch your measurements for strip lengths.

YOU'LL NEED:

MATERIALS:

- Red bond or construction paper 8 ½ x 11"
- Yellow or golden bond or construction paper 8 ½ x 11"

STEPS:

1. Cut red and yellow/gold paper into 1 1/4" x 11" strips

2. Tape each color of strip lengths together in 3's or 4's (depending on wrist size) so you have very long strips of red and yellow/gold.

3. Place just the ends of the strips over each other, into a big "L" 90 degree corner shape, and tape the ends together securely

4. Fold one side down over the square to start alternating the folds

5. Fold the strips over one another in turn, making squares of each color in an alternating pattern

6. When you finish, fold in the ends and tape together to form the bracelet

GRAIN OF RICE

This folding method can also be used to make hanging garlands, pop-up cards, stick puppet bodies or your own creation

Simple Asian Crafts

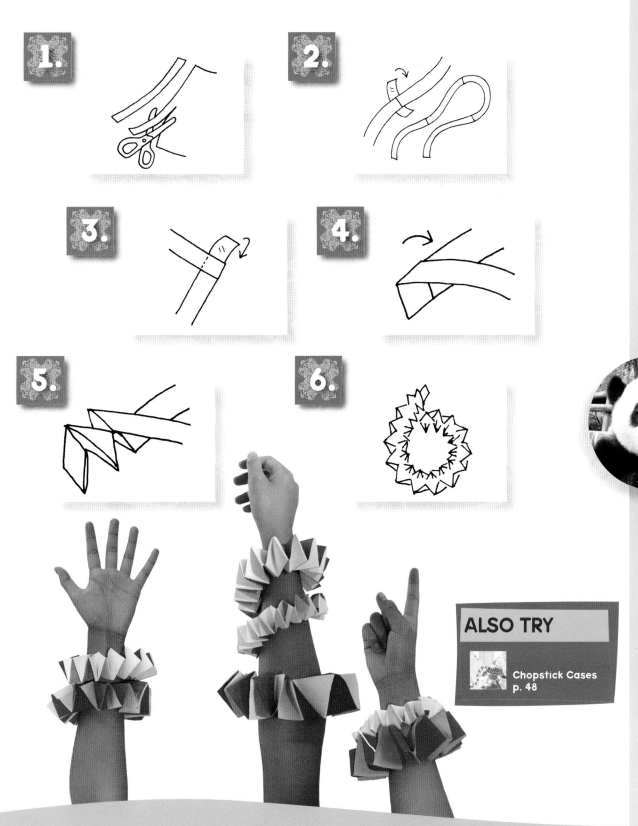

1.

2.

3.

4.

5.

6.

ALSO TRY

Chopstick Cases
p. 48

简单亚洲手工

YO-YO 溜溜球

This is a very simple toy to make and is a non-traditional version of the Chinese yo-yo. It can be a wonderful party favor, small gift or Chinese New Year toy and won't take long to make ahead in a large quantity. Once assembled, you play with the yo-yo by holding the end of the stick and flicking your wrist so the paper coil extends and retracts.

YOU'LL NEED:

MATERIALS:

- Long patterned or gold lightweight paper (wrapping paper works well)

- 10 or 12" dowel or chopstick, or colorful drinking straw

- Paint or other coloring medium

STEPS:

1. Draw or paint stick a bright color (if wood or bamboo) and let dry

2. Cut paper to about 40" x 5" size (adjust depending on stick size)

3. Tape a short end of the paper strip securely so it's even with the top of stick

4. Coil paper tightly, patterned side out

GRAIN OF RICE

You can secure the rolled paper tops with small rubber bands until ready to use to keep them neat and help curl the paper. This will also keep them coiled if you want to store or display them sticking out of a container

TIPS FOR YO-YO FUN

- Try sheet and wrapping papers with different colors and patterns. You can use cool, fun patterns, Asian prints or themed paper

- Get fancy and paint your stick with color and design that goes with your paper

- For a party or event, gather the kids together and make the yo-yos as a group activity

- Have a contest by standing side by side and seeing who can flick their yo-yo the farthest

Simple Asian Crafts

Did You Know?

+ The other type of very different Chinese yo-yo is traditional dating back to the Ming Dynasty. It consists of two discs with an axle connecting them. A performer spins and tosses the yo-yo holding a stick in each hand connected by a string

简单亚洲手工

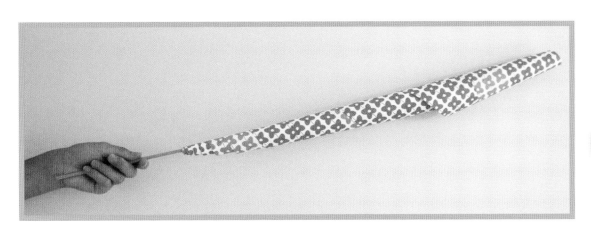

ALSO TRY

Shuttlecock p. 90

Rattle Hand Drum p. 84

GREAT WALL CARD

长城卡

No book about China would be complete without including The Great Wall. It remains one of the world's most amazing architectural achievements. It was built over 2000 years ago during the reign of the first emperor of China, Qin Shi Huang, to protect from invaders from the north. The wall, which was built in sections, curves across the landscape "like a dragon" for over 3700 miles (over 5000 kilometers) covering five provinces and two autonomous regions.

The most visited and well-preserved area of the wall today winds through Beijing, China's capital city. This is partly through restoration but also because it is constructed of mostly brick and stone whereas many of the earliest sections made of tamped earth lie in ruins.

This unique Great Wall card design depicting one of the most recognized historical landmarks in the world can be used for any type of occasion, note, greeting or invitation.

YOU'LL NEED:

 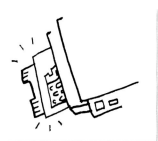

MATERIALS:

• White cover weight stock 8 1/2 x 11"

STEPS:

1. See template on p. 123 and copy or trace on to cover weight paper

2. Color in illustrated side

3. Cut around contour of card following template (only cut around outside edge)

4. Fold on dotted lines with smaller flap in front

5. Place message or artwork inside

6. You can add a tab and slit to the flaps by cutting as shown if you want a closing card or plan to slip anything inside

GRAIN OF RICE

Complete and fold your card before adding your message or decoration. That way you will see what area appears when folded and what area is concealed inside until it is opened.

Simple Asian Crafts

Did You Know?

+ Millions of soldiers, peasants, laborers and prisoners were needed to build the thousands of miles of The Great Wall. Conditions were poor and many died during construction and were buried beside and beneath the wall

简单亚洲手工

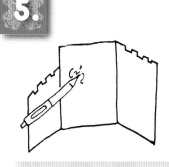

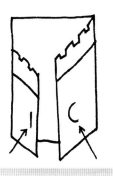

PROJECT RESOURCES

Papercut Designs
pp. 109, 110

Zodiac Animals
p. 111

Celebration Garland
p. 111

Lucky Red Envelope
p. 112

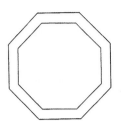

Chopstick Case
p. 113

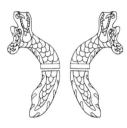

Floating Dragon Boat
p. 114

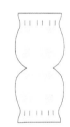

Scented Incense Bag
p. 115

Dragon Puppet
pp. 116, 117

Shadow Puppets
pp. 118, 119

Monkey King Mask
p. 120

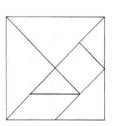

Tangram
p. 121

Climbing Panda
p. 122

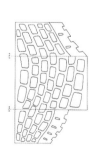

Great Wall Card
p. 123

New Year "Fu" Banner
p. 124

*Trace or copy – do not cut or remove

TEMPLATE
Papercut Designs 剪纸, Double Fish, pp. 22–23

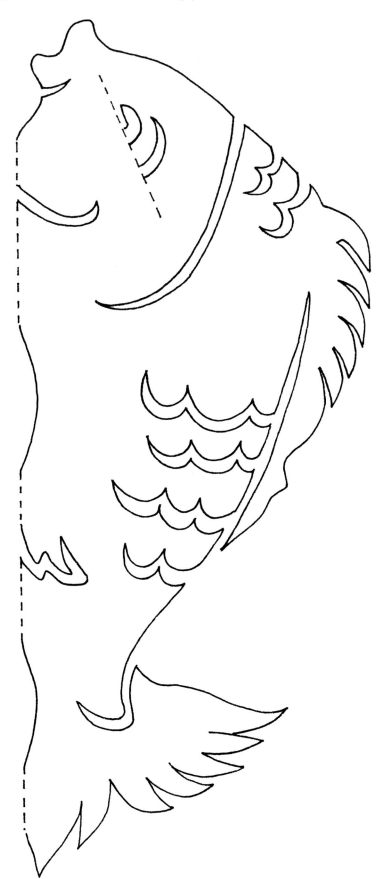

TEMPLATE
Celebration Garland 拉花, pp. 34–35

Zodiac Animals 生肖转盘, Octagon, pp. 44–45

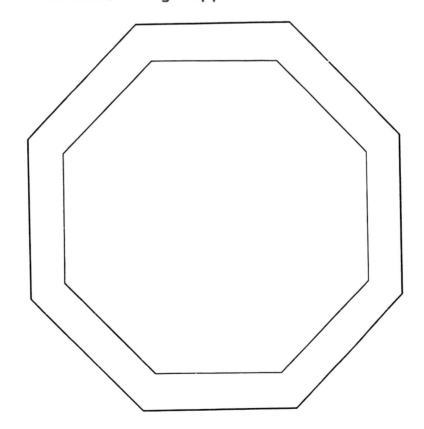

*Trace or copy – do not cut or remove

*Trace or copy – do not cut or remove

TEMPLATE
Floating Dragon Boat 划龙舟, pp. 58-59

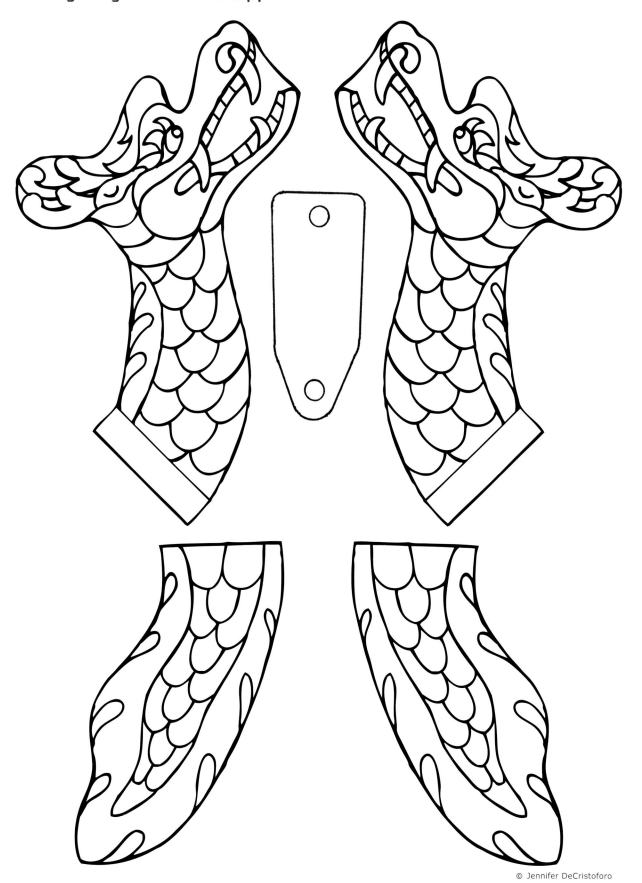

***Trace or copy – do not cut or remove**

© Jennifer DeCristoforo

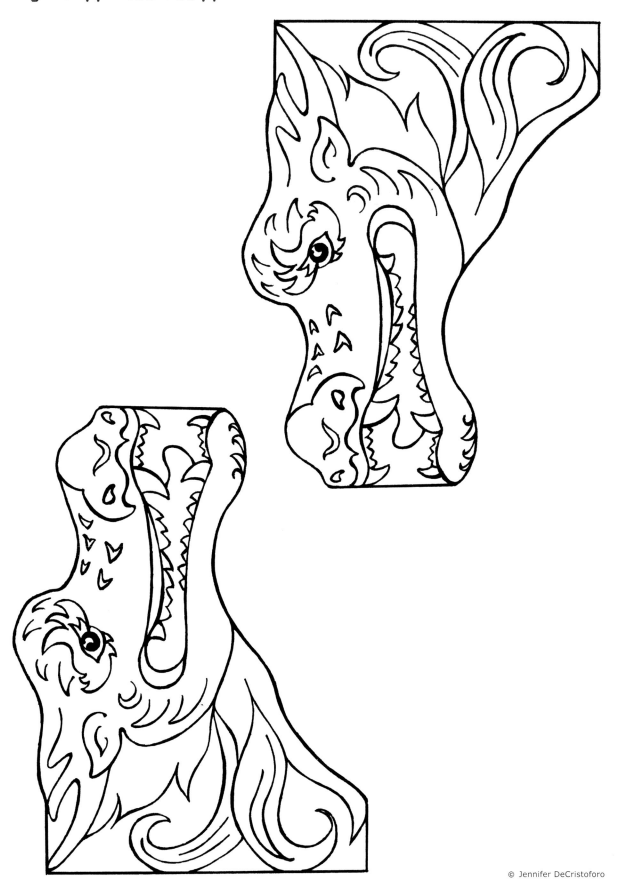

TEMPLATE
Dragon Puppet 龙形木偶, pp. 68-69

*Trace or copy – do not cut or remove   copy at 120%   **117**

L

R

L

R

CUT OUT

L

R

CUT OUT

CUT OUT

*Trace or copy – do not cut or remove

TEMPLATE
Shadow Puppets 皮影戏, pp. 76–79

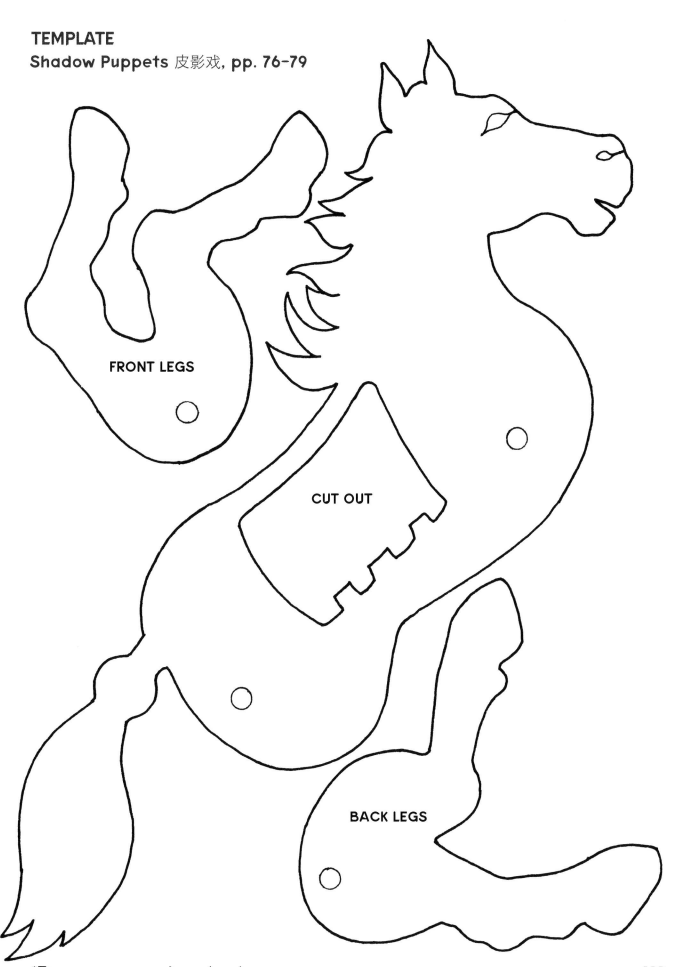

FRONT LEGS

CUT OUT

BACK LEGS

*Trace or copy – do not cut or remove

TEMPLATE
Monkey King Mask 美猴王面具, pp. 80-81

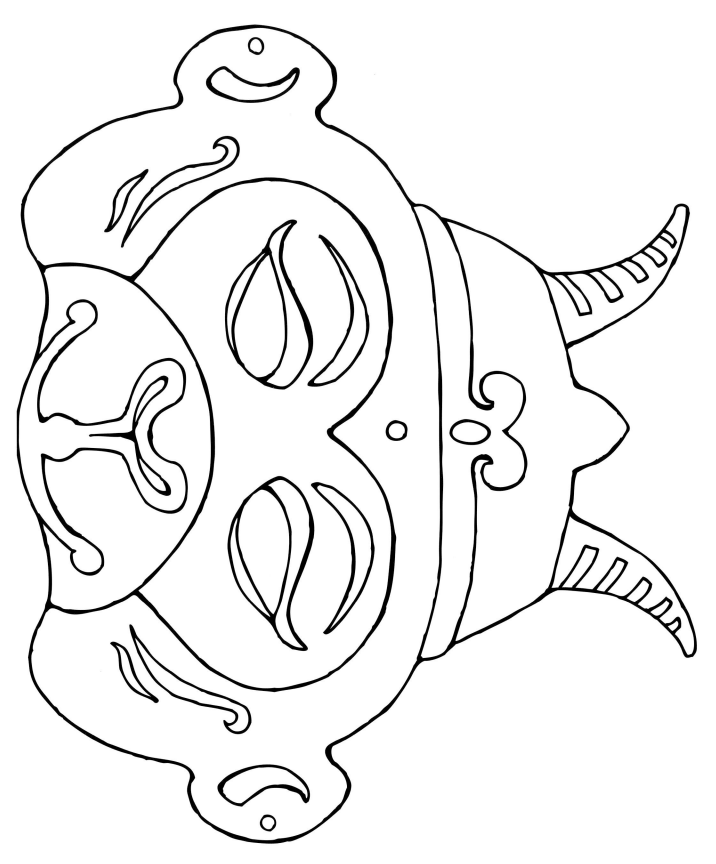

*Trace or copy – do not cut or remove

TEMPLATE
Tangram Pieces 七巧板, pp. 92-93

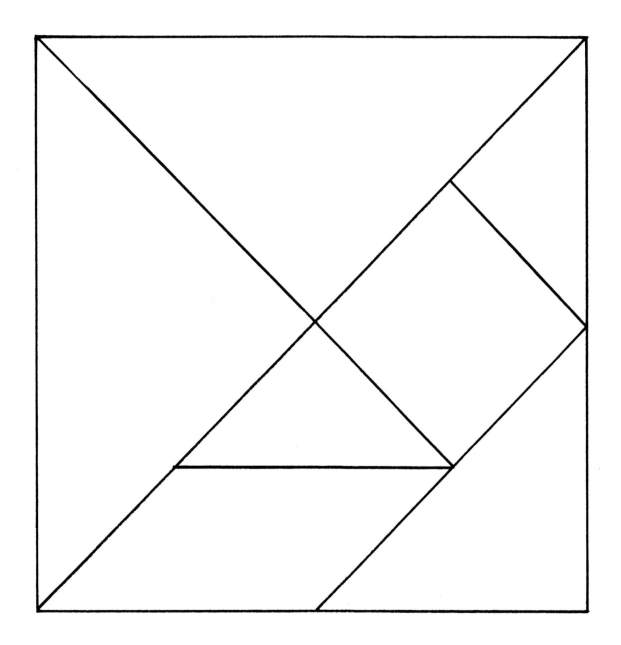

*Trace or copy – do not cut or remove

TEMPLATE
Great Wall Card 长城卡, pp. 104-105

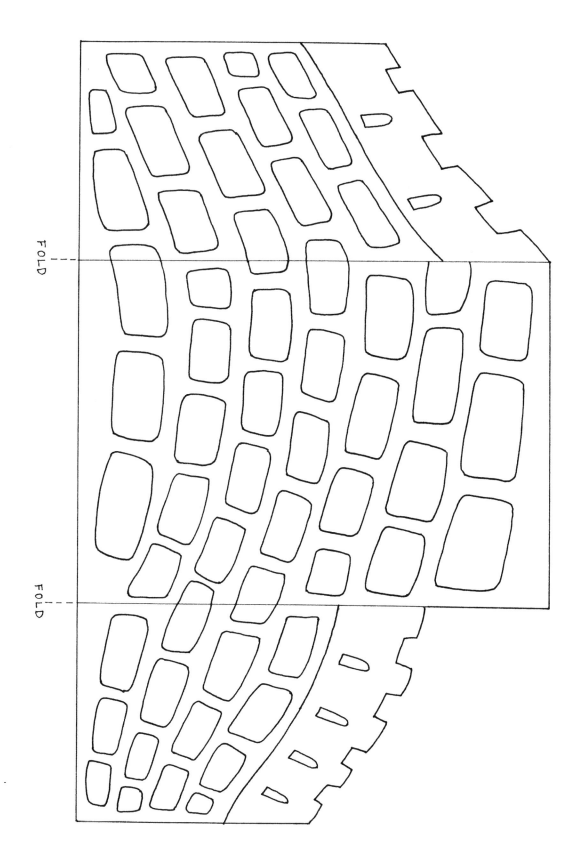

FOLD

FOLD

*Trace or copy – do not cut or remove

copy at 120%

欢声笑语贺新春

欢聚一堂迎新年

合家欢乐

© Jennifer DeCristoforo

*Trace or copy – enlarge to fit doorway

Twelve Zodiac Animals 十二生肖

鼠   牛   虎

兔   龙   蛇

马   羊   猴

鸡   狗   猪

*Trace or copy – do not cut or remove

Dragon Head Parade Diagram p. 36
舞龙的道具服饰

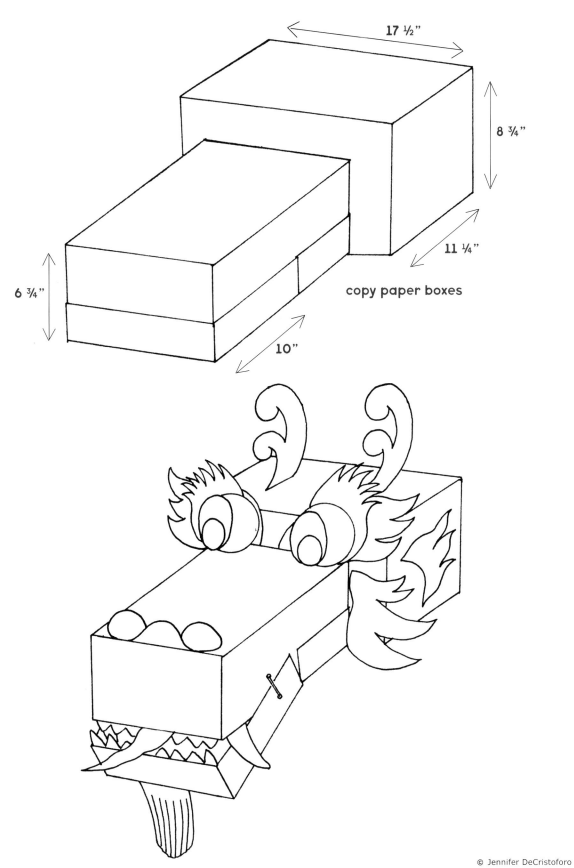

17 ½"

8 ¾"

6 ¾"

11 ¼"

copy paper boxes

10"

Speak and Write Mandarin–
Common Words and Phrases

Hello **nîhăo** 你好
How are you? **nǐhǎo ma** 你好吗
I am fine **wǒ hěnhǎo** 我很好
Goodbye **zàijiàn** 再见
I love you **wǒ ài nǐ** 我爱你

Pardon me **duìbuqǐ** 对不起
Thank you **xièxiè** 谢谢
You are welcome **búyòng xiè** 不用谢
Goodmorning **zǎo ān** 早安
Goodnight **wǎn ān** 晚安

Father **bàba** 爸爸
Mother **māma** 妈妈
Son **érzǐ** 儿子
Daughter **nǔér** 女儿
Older brother **gēge** 哥哥
Older sister **jiějie** 姐姐

Younger brother **dìdi** 弟弟
Younger sister **mèimei** 妹妹
Grandmother **nǎinai** 奶奶
Grandfather **yéye** 爷爷
Teacher **lǎoshī** 老师
Friend **péngyǒu** 朋友

China **zhōngguó** 中国
moon **yuè** 月

mountain **shān** 山
river **hé** 河

One 一 **yī**
Two 二 **èr**
Three 三 **sān**
Four 四 **sì**
Five 五 **wǔ**

Six 六 **lìu**
Seven 七 **qī**
Eight 八 **bā**
Nine 九 **jiǔ**
Ten 十 **shí**

Have a Happy and Prosperous
New Year!

gōngxǐ fācái 恭喜發財

Common Chinese Characters

福

Good Fortune

心

Heart

爱

Love

生命

Life

和平

Peace

勇气

Courage

和谐

Harmony

幸福

Happiness

力量

Strength

Auspicious Chinese Symbols

As you become familiar with Chinese art, handcrafts, objects and architecture from the past and present you will notice the rich symbolism that is included in the designs. Almost everything from nature has some sort of special significance for the Chinese, but these are some of the most common.

You can also reference the Chinese Character section for calligraphy words that are common auspicious messages and the Zodiac Animals for their symbolism.
As you do the crafts in this book, think about how you can include some of these themes and messages so your project has a stronger symbolic meaning and will hopefully attract good fortune!

BUTTERFLY- love
CARP- abundance, prosperity
CRANE- nobility, honesty, longevity, peace
DRAGON- power, good fortune and success, self-confidence
GOLDFISH- happiness, wealth, wisdom
LOTUS- love, harmony, purity
PEACH- longevity
PHOENIX- happiness, peace, luck, kindness, compassion, glory
PEONY- prosperity, wealth, honor
TIGER- good fortune, prosperity

Easy Shuttlecock Games (Jian Zi) p.90

One person games:
- Throw the shuttlecock up in the air, then keep it up using only your sides of feet to kick. See how long you can keep it going before it hits the ground

- Now try keeping it up in the air with just your knees

- Now try alternating between your feet and your knees, and between left and right, too!

Two person game:
- How about playing with a friend? One of you throws the shuttlecock up in the air, and the other kicks it back. How many times can you pass the shuttlecock between you?

Group games:
- Play with more than 2 people; stand in a ring and see if you can keep the shuttlecock in the air using only your feet, passing it around the ring

- Take turns putting one player in the center of the circle and pass it from the center out and back each time. When the center player misses, it's the next turn

- One person throws the shuttlecock high into the air and calls out the name of the person who should kick it next. That person kicks it as high as possible too, calling out the next player, and so on

(Tip to remember- to play the traditional games, no hands allowed!)

ACKNOWLEDGMENTS

The process of creating this book began long before the first word was written and first craft came to life. Too many to name have joined me on my journey as I have grown as a teacher, artist, designer, art director, traveler, crafter, student, mom, and now, published author. I am extremely grateful to all that have collaborated with me in even the smallest of ways and helped me realize this dream.

To all my friends at CAFAM (Chinese & American Friendship Association of Maine), the many years of friendship you have given to me and to Cloe have kept me inspired, active, and proud to be a Chinese-American family. I have learned and gained so much from being part of this community, and have been put to the challenge with designing crafts, teaching, planning events and steering projects, which is all reflected in so much of this book.

Frank Berté and Emma Lockwood, you are wonderful to work with and added so much more than design and production services. Thank you both for immersing yourselves into this project with your creativity, feedback, patience and dedication. Every page of this book has benefited from your talents, skill and careful attention.

My heartfelt thanks to my friend Yuyang You. Your indispensable advice and ideas for this book have made an incredible difference in the authenticity and quality of the projects, and my increased understanding of Chinese culture. From beginning to end you were always willing to help and were so generous with your time and knowledge.

To all my family members and friends, your check-ins and support over these "book" years were the fuel I needed to keep on and keep getting better. Your enthusiasm every step of the way has been incredibly appreciated. Tammy and Zabrina, Elena, Sally, Eliza and Wendy, you have been my special champions and were always there to hear about my latest foray with scissors and glue.

Lastly and most importantly, thank you Cloe. This book would not have been written without the purpose you bring to it and your unconditional love. From scrutinizing the projects to being a "hand model", you exist in every aspect of this book and the book exists because of you.

Tips for Parents and Educators:

MATERIALS TOOLBOX
As you get crafting, you will find there are tools and materials you want to always keep on hand. The tools can be found on p.7. Here are some good basic materials:

Construction paper	Tracing paper
Colored craft foam	Colored duct tape
Variety of paints	Clear packing tape
Plastic straws	Fabric
Poster board	Chenille stems
Tag board	Glitter
Colored gift tissue	Beads
Cords, ribbon, string	

TRASH TO TREASURE
These are some of the recyclables used in the craft projects that you can start saving now:

Newspaper	Plastic tubs and lids
Scrap paper	Gift wrap tubes
Corrugated cardboard	Bath tissue tubes
Cereal boxes (to cut patterns)	Quart milk/juice cartons

AT HOME
If you are new to crafts, peruse this book first and select some of the easier skill level crafts while you build your confidence and learn the format of the instructions.

Designate a "go to" area in your home for craft materials and supplies. (Remember to keep toxic or potentially dangerous supplies in a less accessible place!) It will be easier to plan your project knowing what you have, and it also lets your kids know you value your creative time together.

Allow your children's natural creativity to stray from the directions or design to see where they land. You can always start over!

IN THE CLASSROOM
Many of these crafts can be integrated into a full lesson plan. Tangrams, calligraphy, the abacus and kite making are just a few of the projects that can easily be expanded into longer units. Explore ideas for language arts, science, history, world cultures, mathematics, etc. that bring more depth of knowledge to the topic, or partner with other teachers, particularly if you are meeting a learning objective.

The internet is an obvious source for planning with additional research but also have it available during your craft process. Having a tablet nearby is helpful for fielding questions or looking up tips if you experience setbacks.

Allow your students to approach the craft with different learning styles. Some will insist on being very specific about following the steps; others will want to dive in, jump ahead or go off the path. This negotiation can be a challenging yet rewarding part of your teaching process. Working in mixed level smaller groups can also foster creativity and collaboration.

Think about the steps and plan ahead for the time involved. You may need to divide some of the projects into a few short sessions. Also, build in the time for your students to display, present or use their completed craft.

If you are in a region with great, warm weather always consider taking the messier projects outside. Just keep in mind the closest water source. You can leave the projects in the sun to dry quickly.

During clean up, have plastic containers with lids on hand for extra materials and paint. Also make sure there is a storing and drying area cleared for the projects before you finish!

FOR LARGE EVENTS:

Put some serious thought into estimating the likely amount of guests so you don't go way over or way under on materials and craft templates.

Evaluate your craft materials based on your group. For instance, acrylic craft paint and black India ink work beautifully for some projects but if you are going to have many young children or uncertain supervision at open tables, use all non-toxic, non-staining materials.

When the December holiday season is approaching stock up on craft materials and decorations to save for your Chinese New Year event! Red is everywhere in copy/card paper, gift bags, streamers and table coverings. Also look for metallic gold decorations, gift wrap and tissue and red & gold twinkle lights.

For Chinese New Year, the zodiac animal and character for the celebrated year (p. 126) can be put on a bag, bookmark, headband, fan, stick puppet or your own creation in addition to the decoration craft on pp. 44-45.

You will need a takeaway plan, especially if kids are doing several crafts. Supplying a small paper tote bag works well. It can also be a "bonus" craft to decorate or you can adhere a copied paper design or information about your organization to the front panel.

iNDEX

(g. indicates within 8 pp. Gateway to China section)

Additional Resources and Information

These are websites that I have found useful for products, education and information. I can't personally guarantee and am not responsible for the accuracy of their information, the quality of their products and services or the longevity of their active links.

Diamond Kite pp. 86-87
Weifang World Kite Museum
http://www.wfworldkitemuseum.com/en/index.aspx

Climbing Panda pp. 96-97
WWF Global
http://wwf.panda.org/what_we_do/endangered_species/giant_panda/

Chengdu Research Base of Giant Panda Breeding
http://www.panda.org.cn/english/

Chinese Culture
Cultural China- http://www.cultural-china.com/
ChinaCulture.org- http://www.chinaculture.org/

Fine Art and Crafting Supplies
(retailers for art supplies including brushes, paper, paint and ink)

Artist & Craftsman Supply- http://www.artistcraftsman.com/
18 retail stores nationwide as well as online

Dick Blick- www.dickblick.com/

Asian Cultural Products
ChinaSprout- http://www.chinasprout.com/
Pearl River- http://www.pearlriver.com/

Image Credits

g.2 globe map- Shutterstock; g.8 farmers- Creative Commons Attribution- Share Alike 2.0 Generic License; p. 13 Chinese porcelain picture by Peter Griffin- Public Domain Pictures.net; p. 30 dragon dance costume- Brent Wong/ Shutterstock.com; p. 31 red lantern- Shutterstock; p. 31 dragon boats- Shutterstock; p. 85 children playing- Shutterstock; p.105 Great Wall- morguefile; cover- green bamboo- iStockphoto; tab pp. 63-81 lion head- iStockphoto

All other photographs and illustrations are by Jennifer DeCristoforo or are from an available non-licensed collection

Every effort has been made to locate all copyright holders of material used in this book. If any errors or omissions have occurred, corrections will be made in future editions.

Lucky Bamboo Crafts, P.O. Box 1022, Yarmouth, ME 04096
www.luckybamboocrafts.com info@luckybamboocrafts.com © 2013 Jennifer DeCristoforo